T0193117

Releasing *the* *Overcomer's* Anointing

POWER TO OVERCOME

A Guide Outlining How to Survive Challenges, Failure, Poverty,
Disappointment, and So Forth by Taking and Maintaining Victory

Victory Is Yours—Take It!

DR. DARNELL WHYMNS

WESTBOW
PRESS®
A DIVISION OF THOMAS NELSON
& ZONDERVAN

WestBow Press books may be ordered through booksellers or by contacting:

WestBow Press
A Division of Thomas Nelson & Zondervan
1663 Liberty Drive
Bloomington, IN 47403
www.westbowpress.com
844-714-3454

Scripture taken from the King James Version of the Bible.

ISBN: 978-1-6642-3320-1 (sc)
ISBN: 978-1-6642-3321-8 (hc)
ISBN: 978-1-6642-3322-5 (e)

Library of Congress Control Number: 2021908745

Print information available on the last page.

WestBow Press rev. date: 8/18/2021

CONTENTS

FOREWORD

The COVID-19 pandemic challenges people, especially Christians, to change their lifestyles in God. I was very afraid when COVID-19 began spreading worldwide, even as Christian worker. Being that I am a Christian, I was disappointed at my attitude toward the coronavirus, not in the virus itself. The problem is in me as a Christian, not in a virus. Why do I fear? It is because I have not lived holy in God.

God said, "Speak to all the congregation of the children of Israel, and say to them, 'You shall be holy: for I the Lord your God am holy'" (Leviticus 19:2).

To overcome the death problem, one must live in God; that is, one must be holy, which is God's character. The actual manifestation of holiness is Jesus's love.

The Bible tells us of the love that God has toward us, and we have known and believed in this love. God is love; and he who dwells in love dwells in God, and God in him (1 John 4:16).

Love makes us overcome the physical gate of death by following Jesus's example. Complete submission to God makes us holy and thankful in this challenging situation with COVID-19.

Holiness should be activated in our lives, just as the love of God came true through Jesus's coming into the human world.

In the Bible we read, "For where envying and strife is, there is confusion and every evil work" (James 3:16).

Again, to overcome the problem of disease and death, believers should change their lifestyles by following the holy life of God, both spiritually and physically, from now on.

Release the Overcomer's Anointing, written by Darnell Whymns, notes "complete submission to His perfect will" as the holy lifestyle. Her writing will help people succeed in holy living, serving as a guide to showing obedience to God Himself. She stresses that "nothing meaningful ever happens when we partially submit to divine guidance." I think that God permitted this dreadful COVID-19 situation because we have just partially submitted ourselves to Him spiritually and physically. In the way of actual and complete following of God's holy life, *Release the Overcomer's Anointing* is a good guide to overcoming this sinful and imperfect world, moving onto glorious eternal life in heaven with God.

Pastor Taikoo Chang
Grace Church (Foreigners Mission)

PREFACE

To overcome is the divine right of the believer. The ability to break a cycle is of God and can only be realized by His favor and directive. To obtain this ability from God—even though, being God, He gives it to whom He wills—one must be free from sin. There must be no misguided truth about receiving anything from God.

God is holy and requires all who acknowledge Him as Lord to be like Him, holy. He spoke about putting new wine into old bottles. To release victory, the source and the destination must have the same characteristics. Otherwise, there just might be a malfunction. The principles of righteousness are to function in righteousness (right living). The scripture explains it this way by asking an important question: "Can two walk together, except they be agreed?" (Amos 3:3).

We need not be deceived by sin. However, the choices we make determine how effectively we will live for God's glory. They determine how and if we overcome. God is looking for His Word, and He can only respond to His Word. He is His Word. The quality of our success, then, is in our submission to Christ.

"Can two walk together, except they be agreed?" (Amos 3:3). There must be an agreement. Sin refutes righteousness and therefore will not permit the perfect will of God for our lives to become evident. However, we should live righteously, our lives being a living complement to the Word of God. When such is the case, God is able to release His Word concerning us, and we will be changed.

It is by divine instruction that I write as God's Holy Spirit dictates. He insists that each of us studying the pages of this text understand that the first requirement for His intervention in any of our challenges is complete submission to His perfect will. We must give our lives to Him in all holiness.

This manual will be the guide between obedience and the manifestation of God Himself in our lives. It serves to motivate, educate, and guide and to release the power of God through its pages.

Again, I stress the fact that nothing meaningful ever happens when we partially submit to divine guidance. Partial submission will yield a partial solution. Newton explained it this way: "For every action, there is an equal and opposite reaction." However, with God we know that if we are lukewarm, He will reject us. We must be complete and uncompromised to get God's favorable response.

"So then because you are lukewarm, and neither cold nor hot,
I will spew you out of my mouth" (Revelation 3:16).

ACKNOWLEDGMENTS

I wish to thank the Lord, who alone is full of wisdom, knowledge, and might. He is wisdom Himself. The revelation behind our victory as documented in *Releasing the Overcomer's Anointing* is from Him as He has revealed. He has indeed made His power to accompany His every instruction. I am grateful for every trial and every challenge that He allowed me to go through to verify the truth found in this text.

I am also grateful for my family members (my husband, David; son, David Jr.; and daughters, Davielle and Danielle) who have been co-laborers. Together we have tested and proven every word in this text and have found them to be all true and sure as the Lord would have said. The encouragement and motivation of my family has inspired me to continue to press on in God's presence. Consequently, God has revealed Himself and released miracles. I am truly grateful.

Amen.

INTRODUCTION

Release the Overcomer's Anointing was written because the devout people of God all over the world poured out their hearts before God in prayer, asking for a way out of the hands of the enemy. Even as I write, this scripture overwhelms the ear of my spirit:

> This poor man cried, and the Lord heard him, and saved
> him out of all his troubles. (Psalm 34:6)

God cares and so has charged me to both write and teach this victory, by activating it in your physical reality.

To teach this topic successfully, the instructor must have had an experience where all the principles discussed herein were actively carried out successfully. It is only then that the ability to convey this divine breakthrough is possible. For it is the trial of our faith that works patience, and it is suffering that gives birth to victory. And this is a victory that is transferable supernaturally.

Successfully tried faith in God moves the believer to this position of triumph. Another person would simply be "reading the letter." I testify to you that the years of struggle and hardship that I have endured have forced me to prove the contents of *Release the Overcomer's Anointing*. It is within this period that the Lord gave me these instructions. Again, I testify that He, by His power, has delivered me.

While passion will serve as the catalyst for delivery of this divinely instructed manual, prayer of both the presenter and the student will marry faith to serve as the catalyst for victory over individual circumstances. We must remember that we cannot perform tasks and expect that God will be manipulated into giving us what we desire. True victory is not manipulated. It comes as we become intimate with God.

He takes the wise in their own craftiness: and the counsel of the fraudulent is carried headlong. (Job 5:13)

Yes, and all that will live godly in Christ Jesus shall suffer persecution. (2 Timothy 3:12)

There is no getting around it. The challenge is to make it through the obstacles with consistency in Christ. We are expected to exemplify, in spite of the heavy press, Christlike characteristics with thankfulness and without compromise. Our home is not here, and in pursuit of our heavenly abode there will be challenges. We must be reminded daily that we may be in the world but not of the world.

They are not of the world, even as I am not of the world. (John 17:16)

We are not obliged in the least to this world. Should we feel as though we are in debt to it, we will find ourselves in sin simply because we are reluctant to come out of it. We must come out—that is, die—so that we might live. Daily we must put on the whole armor of God.

Put on the whole armor of God, that you may be able to stand against the wiles of the devil.

For we wrestle not against flesh and blood, but against principalities, against powers, against the rulers of the darkness of this world, against spiritual wickedness in high places.

Why take to you the whole armor of God, that you may be able to withstand in the evil day, and having done all, to stand.

Stand therefore, having your loins girt about with truth, and having on the breastplate of righteousness;

And your feet shod with the preparation of the gospel of peace;

Above all, taking the shield of faith, with which you shall be able to quench all the fiery darts of the wicked.

And take the helmet of salvation, and the sword of the Spirit, which is the word of God:

Praying always with all prayer and supplication in the Spirit, and watching thereunto with all perseverance and supplication for all saints. (Ephesians 6:11–18)

But as many as received him, to them gave he power to become the sons of God, even to them that believe on his name. (John 1:12)

We must understand that everything we experience in life might be the consequence of decisions we have made. Most certainly there are desires and longings that may not be the best ones to follow through with and act upon. Yet oftentimes we do just this. This choice to act is ours, not another's. Therefore, we should not seek to blame anyone but ourselves. The issues of life flow from the heart. Issues, then, can be considered to be those challenges we face: difficulty in relationships, financial hardships, self-control, mind battles, and so many other matters.

Keep your heart with all diligence; for out of it are the issues of life. (Proverbs 4:23)

Everything we experience daily has come from our hearts. We desired certain things, and therefore we made decisions accordingly. Some of those decisions drew us to God; some drew us far from Him, in which case it is for us to soberly return to the old landmark.

Finally, as you read each chapter, meditate on the scriptures. They are included as a reminder of the promises God has given to us through His son's ultimate sacrifice and evidence to verify that He is true. Each chapter concludes with a prayer and declaration. It is recommended that you pray each pray as a personal conversation between you and our Father in addition to repeating each declaration as an individual statement of faith. The prayer is a guide to affirm our faith and align each reader with the truth of God's word. The declaration is a confession of the reader's acceptance of this truth and an instrument of motivation to accept this truth as a principle in overcoming each challenge that life presents.

CHAPTER 1
Let Go of Everything

Yea doubtless, and I count all things but loss for the Excellency of the knowledge of Christ Jesus my Lord for whom I have suffered the loss of all things and do count them but dung that I may win Christ.

—Philippians 3:8 (KJV)

We have come before the King of kings to inquire of Him and ask for His intervention. He demands of us that we understand that all things exist by His instructions alone. He is the Creator and Sustainer of all things. There is nothing we need to bring or add to our circumstances, except to trust His divine wisdom. Oftentimes we are in need of God's help because we might have made mistakes along the way and may be in a position where our present is worse than where we began. For a transforming experience, one would be wise to walk out of everything.

If it is not possible to drop everything, then ask for God's wisdom. He alone can give the answer to unique situations. It is important, however, not to carry our situations; they will only continue to be burdens. By dropping everything, we can position ourselves to hear what God has to say about our situations. The reality is clear: we have been carrying the burdens, challenges, disappointments, dilemmas, and failures for very long, and nothing has worked in our favor. So leaving our challenges, hearing from God, and seeking a new directive may help stimulate a pulse in our circumstances.

Adjusting circumstances while trying to forge ahead is always overbearing, especially if the challenge is difficult. This can be static and depressing. An excellent example to reflect on is the contrast between purchasing an existing building and building a new one. The existing building comes with challenges that have appeared with use. These are not necessarily all known to the purchaser. A new construction allows for an informed position from the inside out. The challenges that might arise would be known and determined based on the method of construction and choices made in the process. In renovation, many things may present themselves in the process that have to be addressed by trial and error—not as much information in this case. This will be costly and prevent timely completion of the project.

There may be situations involving family or our employment where we should definitely consult the Lord before we do anything. He alone can tell us what to do, when to do it, and for how long. It is important to operate in wisdom at all times in spite of our emotional or physical dilemmas. We can look at this process as casting off the thing that prevents us; separating ourselves from the obstacles that we do not necessarily have to address immediately or at all.

> Casting all your care on him; for he cares for you. (1 Peter 5:7)

Give Everything to God in Prayer

It is important to understand that in committing our circumstances to God, we relieve ourselves of the burden that those circumstances place on us. This is most important to understand in fighting for or seeking victory. We do not have to bear the pain or weight associated with our circumstances. This is a promise made by the Lord.

> And fear not them which kill the body, but are not able to kill the soul: but rather fear him which is able to destroy both soul and body in hell. Are not two sparrows sold for a farthing? and one of them shall not fall on the ground without your Father.
>
> But the very hairs of your head are all numbered. (Matthew 11:28–30)

Not only is He a yoke-destroying Savior, but also He, in compassion, sustains the believer through every challenge. This is why He says:

> There has no temptation taken you but such as is common to man: but God is faithful, who will not suffer you to be tempted above that you are able; but will with the temptation also make a way to escape, that you may be able to bear it. (1 Corinthians 10:13)

He has the solutions. He understands our beginnings and our ends. We need only to take His Word to be true and find peace in His assurance.

> Casting down imaginations, and every high thing that exalts itself against the knowledge of God, and bringing into captivity every thought to the obedience of Christ. (2 Corinthians 10:5)

Remember to release the entire situation to Him. Your thoughts should also be free from the burden of the challenges. If you find yourself still overwhelmed by your challenges, then you should consider whether you really gave the matter to God in the first place. To say "I place my family in Your hands, Lord," and still battle moments of depression because there is little or no food is not committing everything. If you look at a sick child and believe in healing but cry at the same time because the finances for the tests needed aren't there, then you've put only some of the situation in God's hands and kept part of it for human intervention. It can prove catastrophic to respond to situations using human intellect or initiatives. The believer is encouraged to be led by the Spirit of God. After prayer and surrender, it would help to look for and expect an answer rather than being perplexed by the severity of the challenges. There is hope.

> For as many as are led by the Spirit of God, they are the sons of God. (Romans 8:14)

The scriptures further admonish the born-again Christian to give everything to God. This is the route to a sure victory.

> Commit your way to the Lord; trust also in him; and he shall bring it to pass.
>
> And he shall bring forth your righteousness as the light, and your judgment as the noonday.
>
> Rest in the Lord, and wait patiently for him: fret not yourself because of him who prospers in his way, because of the man who brings wicked devices to pass. (Psalm 37:5–7)

This act, giving all our cares to God, evokes God's divine guidance and overshadowing. God gives peace for every challenge and guarantees victory. For the believer, faith and prayer will begin to release the breakthrough needed to overcome. God fights for the believer. Once He is acknowledged, He then manages the battle and unveils a path for victory. The believer need only respond in obedience. There are countless testimonies of believers who were directed by the Lord and were happy they obeyed. Obeying God's directives proves extremely helpful when the solution is unknown because the situation is new and uncharted.

For a person in such a position, no experience or education can provide support. This is truly a time to ask for supernatural help. I recall an experience I had trying to complete professional responsibilities on a deadline and the printers were limited. Adding to the challenge, there was a queue to print. One of the staff interrupted my print job to speed up the completion of his own. I knew nothing about network printing at the time. I exclaimed, "What happened!" He said nothing. So, I prayed and I received instructions from the Lord to unplug one cord and connect another. I did this, and my work continued printing! Apparently, the staff member had switched the cords to allow his work to print first. His printer must have malfunctioned. It was not until years later, working with computers more directly, that I understood God's instructions to me. If I had relied on my knowledge, I would not have completed that task in a timely manner because I simply did not know what to do.

According to Saul A. McLeod, the brain has the capacity to process numerous thoughts simultaneously. McLeod elaborates by asserting that the brain has the ability to focus based on goals. Broadbent's filter model (1958), Treisman's attenuation model (1964), and Deutsch and Deutsch's late selection model (1963) are all models of attention. These psychologists studied the ability of individuals to process information. It is their opinion that there is a noted response of selected attention when one is presented with multiple sources of information simultaneously.

The conclusion of the matter is simple: the fewer things to process, the easier it will be to focus on following a clear path out of circumstances that are not meant to take us where God wants us to be.

Hold on to Nothing

Why come out from among them, and be you separate, said the Lord, and touch not the unclean thing; and I will receive you.

And will be a Father to you, and you shall be my sons and daughters, said the Lord Almighty.

—Corinthians 6:17–18 (KJV)

Oftentimes when a boat is sinking in a movie, the characters come to the conclusion that the vessel needs to be lighter. Someone then begins to look for items that are not as valuable or critical to the survival of the passengers and tosses them into the water. Sometimes even food items that are a necessity have to be discarded. This approach needs to be considered when charting a course through challenging circumstances. Some things in life may have no direct penalty, but others, once released, may cause severe loss.

It is important to think clearly and consult the Holy Spirit in order to make prudent decisions. A trusted confidant or counselor may be helpful too. Otherwise, present your concerns in prayer and in fasting before the Lord, if you decide to do so.

Do not make any life-changing decisions swiftly or without guidance. Oftentimes haste creates regret. The point of the effort in dropping everything is not to add sorrow but to move into the restfulness of God. Counsel from more than one person is always wise. However, divine instructions are sure. Notwithstanding, there may be situations that demand an immediate response. Do this prayerfully, trusting that God will honor you and cover you in the decisions you make. Once we acknowledge Him, somehow He has a way of making all things work together for our good.

The important thing is to ensure you drop or release everything that God instructs you to in the manner that He insists. Some things are released incrementally; some, all at once. Some are released permanently or temporarily. At this point, it is important to listen and obey, simply because getting out of troubles is not an easy initiative. To add additional challenges is not prudent. This process is not one of elimination but one that defines the direction forward. The wrong decision can prolong the time or complicate matters further. So, check and recheck to ensure that everything you need to loosen is loosed. Do not hold on to anything you need to say goodbye to.

Once this step has been finalized and executed, the obvious becomes a reality. The multiple distractions or activities that may have been a burden or may have consumed time are now no longer there to prohibit advancement.

This process of prioritizing or elimination frees up time. This time now can be used to find solutions and follow God's instructions to your breakthrough.

*   *   *

Prayer

Father, in the mighty name of Jesus, I come asking Your intervention. I acknowledge every unnecessary weight. I agree that some are of a spiritual nature and others are physical. I repent and ask Your forgiveness for being a host to such things that You have not purposed for me.

It is my request that You move in my affairs and cause me to see those things that You have ordained to take me to the next level in You as priority. Those that You have not ordained to be in my life, reveal them. At this very moment I divorce myself from them. I command that every attachment, whether spiritual or physical, be broken right now in the name of Jesus. I submit my will, my mind, my emotions, and every part of me to Your directive.

Father, I insist that the blood of Jesus seal my liberty from every yoke, every burden, every sin, every piece of baggage—everything that will not perfect Your purpose in my life.

Amen.

Declaration

I declare that every aspect of my life line up with the purpose of the almighty God.

I will walk from this very moment burden-free, in pure liberty that comes from Jesus Christ.

I carry no unnecessary weight going forward, but cast every care on the Lord.

I know He cares and desires the best for me.

I press forward toward the prize because there is a crown that the righteous Judge will give to me.

I receive strength and courage right now in the name of Jesus.

CHAPTER 2
Pray

And he spoke a parable to them to this end, that men ought always to pray, and not to faint;

—Luke 18:1

The believer has a specific purpose for which he or she was created. The details of this purpose can only be revealed if we spend time in prayer, seeking to understand God's will. The more time we spend in prayer, the more details we receive from the Father. Prayer will reveal how close we are to achieving those goals and how far we might have veered from them. Praying draws us to a place where we become more aware of the will of God and where spiritually there is a greater and stronger desire to know more, to experience more of God. This will show us specifically what we need to release to walk in the will of God.

Prayer awakens the spirit of humankind and unleashes the God-given authority of humankind in the earth.

> According as his divine power has given to us all things
> that pertain to life and godliness, through the knowledge
> of him that has called us to glory and virtue. (2 Peter 1:3)

We were created by God for God. We are God's and He is ours. We were created for His pleasure. Prayer reveals who we are, our true identity. Sin has stained us, but through prayer and divine communion, a cleansing takes place and our eyes becomes open to the truth. Our minds are then able to process this truth, and our spirits and bodies align to manifest this truth. Our life is hidden with Christ in God (Colossians 3:3). To expel confusion, we must go to the source of life, Life Himself (Colossians 3:4). In finding and building a relationship with the Father through prayer, we become more aware of who He is. And it is through this mirror that we see ourselves.

I remember some years ago, I was feeling down. It seemed as though the challenges I was facing simply had no end, and I felt worn as a result of the multitude and frequency with which they came. It showed on my face, in my communication, in my health, and in what I did that I really was being defeated. Somehow, I found myself running to prayer, even more continually because of my dilemma. During the process of crying out and asking the Lord for help, deliverance, or simply a way out, I heard clearly a stern but loving response from the Lord.

He did not decline my petition. He also did not declare that He would remove all challenges in an explosion of His greatness because His broken child had gotten His attention. Instead, I understood Him clearly—and I'm still in awe to this day.

I was moved to get up and go to the mirror. Reluctantly, I went and stood in front of the mirror. I did not know what to expect. I stood there.

Again, I was moved to look at myself and understand that I was a no-nonsense woman.

As I gazed in the mirror, I was shocked. I did not see a shy, frail person but a powerful, strong giant of a woman. I understood the following:

1. God was showing me my true nature to bring about His purpose in the earth.
2. I should always see myself the way God sees me because it is who I am.
3. Once I act in the characteristic that God reveals, I will have success. Any other action will frustrate me and encourage insecurity and failure.
4. I should see others the way God sees them.

So, there is a perceived personality and a true personality. One we will never master, and the other we will fit into nicely because it is by divine design.

Later, amid another challenging time, I felt strongly motivated to understand that "prayer still works." Later I was reminded of the power of the blood of Jesus. So quite naturally I plunged into prayer and I saw Him do it. He brought me through it.

This chapter will be the central focus of this text simply because all victory comes from God and follows communication with Him. So, it is imperative that the believer understands and practices daily communion with the Father.

Ask God for Intervention

David had many challenges, many of which we learn about through the Psalms, 1 and 2 Kings, or 1 and 2 Chronicles. One of the things we learn about David is that he continuously called on the name of the Lord. Sin or wrong decisions did not prevent him. He found God especially when he sinned. As a matter of fact, he was very confident that God would hear him and deliver. He stated that when he cried, God heard him and delivered him.

> This poor man cried, and the Lord heard him, and saved him out of all his troubles. (Psalm 34:6)

I met someone years ago who affirmed the value of Christian prayer. She related how she prayed vey earnestly and how her prayers were continuously starting over because she simply wanted to be true to her faith. She further said in disappointment, "Of all those prayers I prayed, not one was answered." With opposition from her family, she later became a Christian. She continued the conversation and told me that sometime in prayer, as a Christian, she was praying, and instantly she saw the vision of three women in prayer. One was a Buddhist, one a Muslim, and the other a Christian. Then again, she saw another. This time the Christian was rejoicing and praising God because her prayers had been answered. The Muslim and Buddhist women were still praying and waiting for an answer from their gods.

This woman's conclusion as a converted Muslim was that God hears and answers prayers. She believes this because she received what she had asked for almost immediately. "This never happened before," she said, "with all those long hours of prayer I prayed."

Repent

Any meaningful prayer we pray must be exercised from within the body of Christ. God is sovereign over all people. This includes all genders, religious persuasions, and races.

> God reigns over the heathen: God sits on the throne of his holiness. (Psalm 47:8).

> Now we know that God hears not sinners: but if any man be a worshipper of God, and does his will, him he hears. (John 9:31)

He created all humankind whether we acknowledge it or not. It is by His grace that we live and move (Acts 17:28).

However, though He rules over the affairs of human beings, to get His attention when we pray, we must be a part of His body. Otherwise we are on the outside looking in. To be a part of His body, we must confess Jesus Christ as Lord. Now we know that God does not hear the prayer of a sinner.

David cried, "Create in me a clean heart, O God; and renew a right spirit within me" (Psalm 51:10). Repentance allows us to dwell in God's presence. It is follows with a decision to completely submit to God's holy order.

> I beseech you therefore, brothers, by the mercies of God, that you present your bodies a living sacrifice, holy, acceptable to God, which is your reasonable service. (Romans 12:1)

Repentance indicates a complete abandoning of past thoughts, actions, and communications that oppose the character of God. We are expected to forsake everything that God disapproves of and submit wholeheartedly to His will.

> Why laying aside all malice, and all guile, and hypocrisies, and envies, all evil speakings. (1 Peter 2:1)

Make a Covenant with God

God honors covenants. He not only responds to covenants but also accepts them as a confirmed negotiated position in our relationship with Him. As He is faithful to keep His position or fulfill His promise, so He expects us to honor our agreement with Him. As Abraham kept his commitment to God, the covenant God made with him thousands of years ago is still honored even among Abraham's descendants who do not regard his God (Genesis 17:1–2).

We must be careful, though, because of the following:

Covenants Are Not Easily Broken

> When you vow a vow to God, defer not to pay it; for he
> has no pleasure in fools: pay that which you have vowed.
> Better is it that you should not vow, than that you should
> vow and not pay. Suffer not your mouth to cause your
> flesh to sin; neither say you before the angel, that it was an
> error: why should God be angry at your voice, and destroy
> the work of your hands? (Ecclesiastes 5:4–6)

Based on the record in the scripture, when making a covenant with God, it
is considered more of an arrangement that supersedes the natural order of
things. God admires faith in His ability to respond as a divine being. He is
not easily moved, and He does take words lightly. He is the very essence of
His Word. He expects us, His image, to be the same. So, when we open our
mouths to "reason" through oral discourse, we must understand that every
word is binding and forms the spiritual envelope to hold the agreement,
literally, for eternity.

There Are Penalties for Forfeiting

> For thus said the Lord God; I will even deal with you as
> you have done, which have despised the oath in breaking
> the covenant. (Ezekiel 16:59)

God honors His Word and expects us to do the same. He moves and
reacts based on its integrity. Thus, He expects us to do the same. There is
absolutely no compromising for this. That's why He admonishes us to let
our conversations be based on His Word and exhorts us to be decided in
matters. He is never pleased when we become uncertain or withdraw our
agreement. He has rules in place to encourage commitment to covenants
with Him.

The Bible records how when Israel sinned against God, they were
punished in several ways. They were a nation with a covenant with God.
As with returning an item to the store after purchase, there may be a
restocking fee or a no-cash-back policy. God has His way.

I am often amazed how biblical principles are applied in businesses and that they are successful once executed properly. Also, I wonder, if we see and know these simple principles to be beneficial, then why are we as believers not masters?

God Honors Covenants

> Know therefore that the Lord your God, he is God, the faithful God, which keeps covenant and mercy with them that love him and keep his commandments to a thousand generations.
>
> —Deuteronomy 7:9

God delights in His children coming to Him and asking for His mercy, pardon, or blessing. Just as with a birth parent, He knows our failures but loves us all the same. In 2018, as I was preparing to travel to London, the Lord spoke profoundly to my spirit. I was overwhelmed and began to cry because I could feel God's emotions.

I was led to pray that God's people would call on Him. I was convinced that I should pray that Christians everywhere would pray directly to God, not to humankind. I felt strongly that God was waiting to hear from us. I felt that He was longing to; He wants to bless His people. However, first we need to just cry out to Him.

What Is Prayer?

Prayer is a spiritual vehicle to directly convey us into the will of God. Prayer is communication with God. It is not a monologue, though sometimes only one party might speak. It is not a forum to simply make demands. Prayer is an engaging dialogue between the believer and the Lord. The Lord calls out to His creation, the believer responds, and thereafter communication continues.

Prayer is releasing God's Word to Him. He said the following:

> So shall my word be that goes forth out of my mouth: it shall not return to me void, but it shall accomplish that which I please, and it shall prosper in the thing whereto I sent it. (Isaiah 55:11)

So why not take Him at his word, literally? I was sharing this scripture some time ago, and the Lord placed a wonderful explanation for it in my spirit to share with the listeners at that time.

The Lord responds to Himself. This is so because He respects and honors the credibility in His existence. His Word is His spiritual code revealed temporally. It documents every part of His existence, and more profoundly, it is living. So, when I have prayed, He has taught me to quote His Word regarding my specific request because this act activates this part of Him on our behalf. His Word is released from our lips and hearts in faith. He honors every part of Himself and guards the integrity of His Word. It is this integrity that affirms His deity and establishes His counsel. So, if we quote His Word, we are simply bringing to His attention His promise, rather than His nature, specifically in that situation. Imagine looking in a mirror. The person you see is you. You will hardly ever not accept the fact that the person you see is the real you. This is what quoting the Word does. When we pray scripture in communication with the Father, it is His language, Himself, that He sees and acknowledges. Naturally, He acknowledges Himself, thus granting a solution to our petition. He will not deny Himself.

What the Lord taught me was to understand that spiritually, the world is constructed on His spoken Word. He is His Word. When we quote His Word, we release Him to go into the literal world and align people and opportunities to bring about change for our good. This process has a time factor that is empowered by the believer's faith but is ultimately dictated to by God Himself. So, in the process of time, the Word returns after moving to the request of the believer and fulfilling the divine will regarding it. This literally completes a cycle. The Word is released; it goes out, aligns with the people and circumstance that would satisfy the petition of the believer, then returns to God. It helps to think of the Word released not as a portion of the Bible as it is but as Jesus Himself, fighting for us.

How Do We Pray?

The focus here is on how to pray to get results. At times we might have to consider how we need a word from God, clear divine instructions, and how we need to be able to reach God without a mediator. The question then is, "How do I reach Him for myself, by myself? What do I do to activate a miracle?" Now we cannot manipulate God to do what we insist. Our supplication must be His will.

Pray the Word. God responds to the Word. Every word from Genesis to Revelation gets God's attention. You may ask, "Why?" There are simple truths to respond to this question that will astonish the casual believer:

- God honors His Word.
- He is His Word.
- His Word will not return to Him void.
- Application of the Word separates us from sin.

    For the word of God is quick, and powerful, and sharper than any two edged sword, piercing even to the dividing asunder of soul and spirit, and of the joints and marrow, and is a discerner of the thoughts and intents of the heart. (Hebrews 4:12)

- His Word rejects lies and casts down imaginations.
- It renews our minds.

How Do We "Pray the Word"?

The Lord ministered this to me so beautifully in prayer that I don't think I will ever forget it. Since that time, I have taught this to my children and the multitude children and adults whom He has allowed me to impact in ministry. I was drawn to the scriptures to find a passage that ministered the solution to a problem that I faced. Let's look at a mother needing to pay the light bill but who has no money to do so. The first thing to consider is that she presented her tithes in the house of the Lord and then paid a few bills, but the money is just not enough. She begins to entreat God. The Lord taught me to find a scripture that would be an example, in this instance, of Him supplying the need of His people. We could get even more specific and find a scripture of God supplying the same need in the scripture. And this is directed by our faith and the will of God.

The second step would be to read and meditate on the scripture. The scripture speaks about faith being activated by the Word of God. Now, after we become familiar with the scripture and commit it to our "heart's knowledge," we can begin to present it back to God in prayer.

We will use this scripture as our prayer reference:

> But my God shall supply all your need according to his riches in glory by Christ Jesus. (Philippians 4:19)

Now let's pray the Word back to the Lord. There is no fixed instruction, but in your prayer, you would personalize this scripture by adding personal pronouns or your name, as follows:

> Father, You are my God. And I am Yours. I believe that no good thing will You withhold from those who walk uprightly. I believe that You will supply all my needs according to Your riches in glory by Your Son Jesus.
>
> So I stand on this word, believing that the finances I need to pay the electricity bill will be provided in the name of Jesus. I know that You will make a way for it to be paid.
>
> Right now, I give You praise and I thank You, Father, for making a way.
>
> In the name of Jesus, I pray.
>
> Amen.

At this point you release everything to God and continuously thank Him for the solution, keeping your spirit tuned in for a response or instructions from Him. This is a simple exercise, yet without faith, it can be extremely complicated. For prayer to be effective, to yield results, favorable or unfavorable, we must believe without hesitation that God will honor our prayer.

For different results, our approach to communion with the Lord would be different. This would be the same as if we were relating to a peer, but with reverence. We understand that there are no restrictions; there are a few guidelines, but otherwise we have open access to the throne room. To celebrate, we would use a different tone and choice of expression from that we would use to ask a favor. So it is with God.

Biblical records show there are situations that merit a different approach to communicating with the Father. It is important to know them in order to have an effective prayer life. Let's have a brief look at a few of these:

Hezekiah's Prayer

> Then Hezekiah turned his face toward the wall, and prayed to the Lord, and said, Remember now, O Lord, I beseech you, how I have walked before you in truth and with a perfect heart, and have done that which is good in your sight. And Hezekiah wept sore.
>
> —Isaiah 38:2–3

1. Hezekiah reminded God of his commitment to walk upright before him. Right standing with God (holiness) will be a witness before God in time of trouble. Abraham obtained God's favor because God equated his faith to righteousness.

   And he believed in the Lord; and he counted it to him for righteousness. (Genesis 15)

2. Hezekiah insisted that God affirm his right standing.
3. He wept. God is moved by our brokenness.

   The sacrifices of God are a broken spirit: a broken and a contrite heart, O God, you will not despise. (Psalm 51:17)

Isaiah

But now, O Lord, you are our father; we are the clay, and you our potter; and we all are the work of your hand.

Be not wroth very sore, O Lord, neither remember iniquity for ever: behold, see, we beseech you, we are all your people.

Your holy cities are a wilderness, Zion is a wilderness, Jerusalem a desolation.

Our holy and our beautiful house, where our fathers praised you, is burned up with fire: and all our pleasant things are laid waste.

—Isaiah 64:8–11

1. Isaiah reminds the Lord that He fathered Israel. No matter how rebellious they were, He was their Father.
2. Isaiah tells the Lord that He made them.

To him the porter opens; and the sheep hear his voice: and he calls his own sheep by name, and leads them out. (John 10:3)

3. Isaiah entreats the Lord for mercy.
4. He outlines the present state of the Israelites.
5. He reminds God of the beauty he once enjoyed from those buildings.

Mary

And Mary said, My soul does magnify the Lord,

And my spirit has rejoiced in God my Savior.

For he has regarded the low estate of his handmaiden: for, behold, from now on all generations shall call me blessed.

For he that is mighty has done to me great things; and holy is his name.

And his mercy is on them that fear him from generation to generation.

He has showed strength with his arm; he has scattered the proud in the imagination of their hearts.

He has put down the mighty from their seats, and exalted them of low degree.

He has filled the hungry with good things; and the rich he has sent empty away.

He has helped his servant Israel, in remembrance of his mercy;

As he spoke to our fathers, to Abraham, and to his seed for ever.

—Luke 1:46–55

1. Mary simply gave God praise.
2. She itemized all His favors.

Pray with divine inspiration. The most effective prayer in this season is the prophetic, where you pray the instruction of God. Pray the will of God as

He orates. When the Lord places something about which you should pray into your spirit, you simply say it again in faith to release it into your life, the life of the subject of your prayer, establishing it in the earth.

What Are the Types of Prayer?

I will not discuss each type of prayer at length but will simply indicate what they are. I will provide further detailed discussions on prayer in my book on prayer, *An Overcomer's Prayer Guide.*

Prayer of Agreement

> Again I say to you, That if two of you shall agree on earth as touching any thing that they shall ask, it shall be done for them of my Father which is in heaven.
>
> —Matthew 18:19

During this prayer, several believers assemble together or agree in principle while praying for a particular matter. They have a common position in God's Word regarding the prayer request, and they pray accordingly. One person may pray aloud while others agree. All parties may pray at the same time, or each person might pray, one at a time.

Prayer of Faith

This prayer is one based on faith; you believe God for something. It can be in agreement with others or as an individual prayer:

> Is any among you afflicted? let him pray. Is any merry? let him sing psalms.
>
> Is any sick among you? let him call for the elders of the church; and let them pray over him, anointing him with oil in the name of the Lord:

And the prayer of faith shall save the sick, and the Lord shall raise him up; and if he have committed sins, they shall be forgiven him.

Confess your faults one to another, and pray one for another, that you may be healed. The effectual fervent prayer of a righteous man avails much.

Elias was a man subject to like passions as we are, and he prayed earnestly that it might not rain: and it rained not on the earth by the space of three years and six months.

And he prayed again, and the heaven gave rain, and the earth brought forth her fruit.

Brothers, if any of you do err from the truth, and one convert him;

Let him know, that he which converts the sinner from the error of his way shall save a soul from death, and shall hide a multitude of sins. (James 5:13–20)

Prayer of Consecration and Dedication

And he was withdrawn from them about a stone's cast, and kneeled down, and prayed, Saying, Father, if you be willing, remove this cup from me: nevertheless not my will, but yours, be done.

—Luke 22:41–42

This prayer is prayed in preparation for service. Jesus prayed in the garden of Gethsemane, asking for the Lord to change the requirement for Him to go to the cross, but knowing that it must be, He submitted.

Prayer of Praise and Worship

When worshipping God or giving Him praise, one makes no requests. That is, we are not asking for money, hope, joy, guidance, or intervention or about any matter of the heart. During this time we simply praise Him for what He has done and for who He is. When worshipping, we take our praise further and adore Him by showering Him with facts about His character.

> And the shepherds returned, glorifying and praising God for all the things that they had heard and seen, as it was told to them. (Luke 2:20)

Prayer of Intercession

During the intercessory prayer, focus on self is to be avoided. It is during this time of prayer that the believer presents the needs of others before the Lord. Sometimes it may be referred to as "standing in the gap." It is the result of the biblical mandate to be stewards to brothers and sisters in Christ.

> I thank my God on every remembrance of you,
>
> Always in every prayer of my for you all making request with joy. (Philippians 1:3–4)

Prayer of Binding and Loosing

When binding and loosing, the believer exercises his or her spiritual authority. A nonbelieving individual may not have such authority. Sin can be an obstacle to getting results from this and any prayer. Spiritual authority, however, can be hindered legally in the spirit by unconfessed sins (Matthew 18:18–19). In this type of prayer, the believer evokes the power of God to restrain the enemy and release the breakthrough that God intends.

Is There a Specific Posture for Prayer?

Different types of prayer will demand varied postures. Here are some suggested positions:

If standing—
- Eyes may be closed with head bowed.
- One may look forward, raising hands up and spreading them. The palms may be up.
- The believer should be looking forward and facing the altar.
- Walk slowly with eyes open.

If lying down—
- Lie on the floor, looking up, with the palms facing up.
- From a position on the floor, face the floor and prostrate.

If sitting—
- While sitting, extend your hands forward with palms facing up.
- While seated, bow your head with eyes closed and hands folded.

If kneeling—
- Fold hands and bow the head.
- Bow, resting the head on the ground, and place hands next to head.

While all the positions and types of prayers are accepted in communicating with the Father, it is devotion, obedience, that will cause us to be effective.

* * *

Prayer

> Father, in the mighty name of Jesus Christ, Your precious
> Son, I come. I confess every sin, known and unknown,

those intentional and not. I ask Your forgiveness and place them all under the blood.

Father, I wish to pray to You, not only to be able to have prayers answered, but also to come to know You and know Your heart. I desire to pray Your will in the earth.

Cause my words in prayer to be Your words; cause my gestures to be Your gestures; cause my groans to be Your groans; and cause my passion to be Yours and Yours alone. Let my prayer shake heaven, earth, and hell with power for Your glory.

I give You all praise for it belongs to You, heavenly Father. I thank You for hearing me and drawing me closer in the name of Jesus.

Amen.

Declaration

I declare that every word out of my mouth in prayer will please God. Every word will agree with the perfect will of God and proceed into the earth to do what it is assigned to do and will not return unsuccessful but will shake the very foundations of the earth. Every word I utter in prayer will act as a two-edged sword, dividing, cutting apart, everything contrary to God's standards. The words I speak in prayer will represent God Himself and cause the enemy to submit, surrender, and abandon all schemes, plans, and assignments established in opposition to the church of God.

There must and will be change and victory as a result of every word I utter in prayer because of the blood of Jesus.

Hallelujah.

CHAPTER 3
Find Your Place in God

Know you not that you are the temple of God, and that the Spirit of God dwells in you?

—1 Corinthians 3:16

Know God Intimately

> Be still, and know that I am God: I will be exalted among
> the heathen, I will be exalted in the earth.
>
> —Psalm 46:10

I have lived and am convinced that the Word I live by is *true*. For it is God himself. No weapon formed against me will ever prosper, and in falling, every dart, every weapon, must flee several ways! God's Word declares it. As a matter of truth, it is His existence. So, I believe it and declare that I live in it! Today join me as I walk in the power of the Word in God Himself! I'm loving it!

He is the spiritual manifestation of His Word. How we exercise our faith will manifest a physical revelation of His presence. This presence brings about change. It is what Jesus Christ came to do in the physical some two-thousand-plus years ago when it was declared that His Word was made flesh.

> And the Word was made flesh, and dwelled among us,
> (and we beheld his glory, the glory as of the only begotten
> of the Father,) full of grace and truth. (John 1:14)

Years ago, the Lord gave me a scripture to study. This scripture spoke to the need for the people of God to begin the journey of understanding who He really is.

> And such as do wickedly against the covenant shall he
> corrupt by flatteries: but the people that do know their
> God shall be strong, and do exploits. (Daniel 11:32)

The information contained in this one verse suggests the following:

1. We know of God (have heard of His existence and the works He carried out on earth).
2. We really do not have an intimate relationship with Him.

3. If we go beyond just being acquainted with Him and endeavor to understand the character and heart of God through His Word and through prayer, then God will manifest Himself in marvelous ways.
4. We would not faint at trials.
5. We would be confident in God's ability to do what we need done.
6. Our faith in God will grow.
7. Miraculous things will take place because of an awakening of our faith.
8. We would walk in divine authority.

To know God, we need to wholeheartedly begin to plunge into the Holy Scriptures. It is impossible to fully understand Him unless we understand what the Word says about his appearance, His likes, His dislikes, how He behaves, what makes Him smile, His lifestyle, His character traits, and His ability. The list goes on. We must consider our approach and be consistent.

His call is for us to have a fulfilling relationship with Him, to know Him in the fullness of His resurrection. He would exhort us to seek to sustain a relationship with God through the good times and when there are rough and even life-threatening circumstances. We should understand that because of the resurrection, we have eternal life. With the mindset that all life comes from God because He is life, we would understand that there is no room for failure. We do not have to defend ourselves. The victory over all opposition is in the blood of Jesus.

> That I may know him, and the power of his resurrection, and the fellowship of his sufferings, being made conformable to his death. (Philippians 3:10)

> Let this mind be in you, which was also in Christ Jesus:

> Who, being in the form of God, thought it not robbery to be equal with God:

> But made himself of no reputation, and took on him the form of a servant, and was made in the likeness of men:

And being found in fashion as a man, he humbled himself, and became obedient to death, even the death of the cross.

Why God also has highly exalted him, and given him a name which is above every name:

That at the name of Jesus every knee should bow, of things in heaven, and things in earth, and things under the earth;

And that every tongue should confess that Jesus Christ is Lord, to the glory of God the Father. (Philippians 2:5–11)

Behold, my servant shall deal prudently, he shall be exalted and extolled, and be very high.

As many were astonished at you; his visage was so marred more than any man, and his form more than the sons of men:

So shall he sprinkle many nations; the kings shall shut their mouths at him: for that which had not been told them shall they see; and that which they had not heard shall they consider. (Isaiah 52:13–15)

This scripture speaks of the approach Christ took when relating to others. He humbled Himself. He knew who He was, but He never sought to make others feel insignificant. He served, and His disciples knew their responsibilities. He acted as a man who had been entrusted with a mandate, not as a God who had infiltrated human culture. For the Lord Jesus, it was more than just an approach; it was who He is.

Become One with God

But he that is joined to the Lord is one spirit.

—1 Corinthians 6:17

If there be therefore any consolation in Christ, if any comfort of love, if any fellowship of the Spirit, if any bowels and mercies,

Fulfill you my joy, that you be like minded, having the same love, being of one accord, of one mind.

Let nothing be done through strife or vainglory; but in lowliness of mind let each esteem other better than themselves.

Look not every man on his own things, but every man also on the things of others.

—Philippians 2

To be one with God is to allow our faith to ascend to the Word of God. It means that everything in the scriptures we believe and, more importantly, are in agreement with. This agreement is demonstrated in our lifestyle. We live based on our conception of how we relate to the world or, more immediately, our communities. Faith is our belief in the Lord when what we believe equals who God is. There is a union. The author of Hebrews stressed to his readers that the effort is in vain to know God if faith is missing:

But without faith it is impossible to please him: for he that comes to God must believe that he is, and that he is a rewarder of them that diligently seek him. (Hebrews 11:6)

Be Grafted In

I say then, Have they stumbled that they should fall? God forbid: but rather through their fall salvation is come to the Gentiles, for to provoke them to jealousy.

Now if the fall of them be the riches of the world, and the diminishing of them the riches of the Gentiles; how much more their fullness?

For I speak to you Gentiles, inasmuch as I am the apostle of the Gentiles, I magnify my office:

If by any means I may provoke to emulation them which are my flesh, and might save some of them.

For if the casting away of them be the reconciling of the world, what shall the receiving of them be, but life from the dead?

For if the first fruit be holy, the lump is also holy: and if the root be holy, so are the branches.

And if some of the branches be broken off, and you, being a wild olive tree, were grafted in among them, and with them partake of the root and fatness of the olive tree;

Boast not against the branches. But if you boast, you bore not the root, but the root you.

You will say then, The branches were broken off, that I might be grafted in.

Well; because of unbelief they were broken off, and you stand by faith. Be not high minded, but fear:

For if God spared not the natural branches, take heed lest he also spare not you.

Behold therefore the goodness and severity of God: on them which fell, severity; but toward you, goodness, if you continue in his goodness: otherwise you also shall be cut off.

And they also, if they abide not still in unbelief, shall be grafted in: for God is able to graft them in again.

For if you were cut out of the olive tree which is wild by nature, and were grafted contrary to nature into a good olive tree: how much more shall these, which be the natural branches, be grafted into their own olive tree?

—Romans 11:11–24

We should be a part of God's body. This is why the church is so effective. We operate with one agenda, one mind, one objective, one body. To be out of the body suggests that we are not functioning the way God designed us to interact. When the Lord grafts the converted individual into the body of Christ, we become just like Him. We live and breathe just like Him. This means there is a union and interaction.

Having a Form of Godliness

Traitors, heady, high minded, lovers of pleasures more than lovers of God;

Having a form of godliness, but denying the power thereof: from such turn away.

For of this sort are they which creep into houses, and lead captive silly women laden with sins, led away with divers lusts,

Ever learning, and never able to come to the knowledge of the truth.

—2 Timothy 3:4–7

There is no way we can seek God and not experience all of who He is. Anyone seeking to only know or experience God partially will simply be acquainted with Him. The reality is the relationship that suggests an intimate connection will not be. We will then speak of Him from what we assume but have not encountered. We know that experience convinces even the doubtful. This experience can only be cultivated in the individual who seeks to be like Christ. Sin is a separating vice. However, consistent devotion to reading and executing the teachings in the Word of God is confirmation of a transformation in progress. It indicates the process of accepting all of God's truth without compromise.

In the process, believers will then not so much deny themselves the opportunity to have Christ cleanse them from all sin but embrace this opportunity to identify with Him. The relationship then is true and pure and not a form or false pretense.

> And has raised us up together, and made us sit together in heavenly places in Christ Jesus. (Ephesians 2:6)

This seat refers to a spiritual position of authority. It speaks of a status of dominance, leadership, and triumph. As a result of a relationship, God invites the believer to assume a position of authority spiritually. This position is demonstrated temporally when we live in accordance with the Word of God.

When we become one with God, we enjoy the benefits of being in His presence. An easy way to understand this is to say that we look just like Him, sharing the same spiritual DNA. We become the image of our Creator. We become His twin with the same opportunities as siblings, the same sense of identity, and the same sense of entitlement. The only thing that limits us is our faith. God will entrust certain privileges to us as long as we commit to His order. We can make requests at the audience of the heavenly Father and insist that they be answered. We speak His Word and watch it transform people, environments, and occurrences for His glory.

Demonstrate His Presence in Our Lives by What We Say or Do

As a result, people are healed, are delivered, and receive Him as Lord and Savior, understanding the mysteries of an all-knowing God. Change in our lives or in the lives of others can only happen when we are in our God-ordained position. Being in position implies we are attentive to the purpose God has for our lives. He gives gifts. It also implies we understand this purpose and that, in obedience to the Lord, we are in the process of fulfilling this purpose. Our relationship with God will determine this call. Some He called, some He predestined. We have not chosen Him, but He has called us and chosen us. His plan is not to have everyone mimicking each other, even though the overall objective of faith in God is the same. There is a unique approach to the manifestation of our purpose and the fulfillment of this purpose. Only the individual believer can carry out this assignment with his or her original sense of humor and temperament. The same applies to every child of God. So, you see, there is an expansive variety of ways to approach one's submission to the lordship of Jesus Christ. He is the author of this complex web. All things that pertain to life and godliness have been authored by His hand.

Just as each of us differs with study habits or preferred meals, our journey to God differs based on our character. Can you imagine telling a person with a choleric temperament to jump and praise the Lord with loud, excited praise? A person with a sanguine temperament might embrace the directive with an elaborate display of emotional adoration. However, the choleric would be just as happy and expressive saying "Thank You, Lord."

Fast, Not So Much for Deliverance but for More of God

> Therefore also now, said the Lord, turn you even to me
> with all your heart, and with fasting, and with weeping,
> and with mourning.
>
> —Joel 2:12

Fasting aligns the human spirit with its Creator. It opens a line of communication that is much more intimate than prayer can do alone. The more frequently the believer fasts, the greater the results will be. It is often said that the more you do something, the better you become at it. This is true with frequent devotion to God. To fast often means the spiritual insight of the believer is strengthened and he or she is keen and alert to communicate with God. What happens during the process of fasting is this:

- Repentance—acknowledgment of transgressions and a complete forsaking of them.
- Interaction with the Word of God—reading, study, meditation, and application.
- Prayer based on the scriptures.
- The seed of the Word is buried into our spirits and we begin to desire more of God.

* * *

Prayer

Father, by Your Word, draw me. Draw me close to Your side. By Your Holy Spirit, lead me to a deeper relationship with You that I might know You in Your fullness. Let me become more and more like You. As I fellowship with You, let Your glory overshadow me that every part of me would be shaped anew in Your image.

Let Your Word fill me so that I will be completely transformed and worthy to sit at Your side, Lord Jesus, in heavenly places, executing heavenly authority.

I give You praise for the privilege.

In Jesus's name, amen.

Declaration

I submit to the perfect will of the almighty God.

I will not identify with another.

For I am His and He is mine.

I acknowledge that I have been bought with a price and that this life I live is Christ living in me. You are my life, Lord.

Right now I align myself with Your will. I rejoice in the fact that I have been grafted into the family of God. I ascend and occupy my seat in heavenly places.

I shall forever be like a tree planted by the river, the river of life.

Amen.

CHAPTER 4
Forgive

Give us this day our daily bread.

And forgive us our debts, as we forgive our debtors.

And lead us not into temptation, but deliver us from evil: For your is the kingdom, and the power, and the glory, for ever. Amen.

—Matthew 6:11–12

Definition of Forgiveness

Forgiveness is "the act of absolving, releasing someone from any obligation, debt."[1]

Explanation

For someone to be forgiven, he or she must have committed an offense. Forgiveness occurs when the offender is pardoned of all offenses.

To the believer, this process means a little more. In criminal justice the records will remain to show the entire process from arrest, to conviction, to the pardoning, then release. The conditions will be documented, along with all evidence for or against the accused. However, in the kingdom of God, the operation is a bit different. When we forgive, we forget. All evidence of any crime is erased and the offender is released with nothing to link him or her to any charge. As a matter of fact, the charge will not exist. The idea is that the blood of Jesus is a very thorough sacrifice for all sins. All guilt and punishment for sin was borne on Calvary's cross. Confession and repentance evoke the power of Christ to forgive sin. This means all sins. The blood, according to Isaiah, washes us and cleanses us of all unrighteousness. So, offenses are absolved by the blood of Jesus.

Absolution is truly a reflection of change with respect to wrongdoings to others, which have been repented of in prayer to the almighty God. God is a righteous Judge and knows how to correct each wayward believer. It is not for us who are seeking holiness and victory to be "teaching people a lesson." This is not scriptural. Such an act is vengeance, and God said that this is reserved for Him.

According to the Lord's Prayer, specifically, "Forgive us our debts as we forgive others their debts," we are expected to be forgiving. Malice, bitterness, guile, and any other emotion suggesting unforgiveness will prevent the process of God's forgiveness from reaching us. The implication in the scripture is that a condition is established by the use of the word *as*. The manner of God's forgiveness of our sins is compared to or equal

---

[1] "Forgiveness," Wikipedia, https://en.wikipedia.org/wiki/Forgiveness, last modified February 2, 2010.

with how we forgive others. This comparison further implies that we must forgive our offender because God will respond to us in the same manner as we do these offenders.

How Do I Forgive?

To forgive, take the following steps:

Acknowledge that You Have Been Offended

It is often said that the first step to defeating a bad habit is to acknowledge that you do have a bad habit. In society we have a practice of refusing to address issues in order to maintain amicable relationships. However, these relationships seem to rest on, or rather cover, offenses. To the public and oftentimes to ourselves, we refuse to accept the fact that we are offended. We want to convey to others that we are great team players with winning attitudes. So, we exchange pleasant greetings and offer cordial responses. However, we may tactfully avoid extended interaction with the person who has offended us.

This is not right. It can lead to denial of the offense because of how we decide to resolve it. We may not wish to approach the person in question, but for our own well-being, we must not pretend as if it did not occur. It is important to accept that we were wronged. This is not to wrong the individual but to understand exactly what the offense is, who did it, why it was committed, and how it was committed.

In this process, you might be careful not to compile evidence of guilt for conviction. But for the process of releasing the individual, you establish all areas where you will not hold him or her guilty. It is a manner of saying, "Yes, this person did all this, but the love of God has washed all of it away, and there is nothing I can hold or am willing to hold as evidence to condemn this person."

In the process, you might find that you were part of the problem, or the Lord might reveal something in your life that you should present before Him. And this begins another opportunity to extend your prayer list. You may now see the offender as a person in need of prayer rather than your wrath. Perhaps you might have initiated the process, or there might be some spiritual attraction in your life that invites such reactions.

It is important to note that each situation is inspired by something previous. This can be a thought (abstract) or a verbal statement, a response, an act, or any gesture.

Repent for Having Held Unforgiveness

Acknowledgment is the beginning of change. It allows us to put a plan in place to bring about change from the foundation of the problem. This process that I propose should indicate the causes and effects. Consider documenting this in tables for self-improvement.

Offense	Offender	Reason	Influence/ motivation	Response	History/ underlying issue	Other
Summary						
Conclusion						
Cause of action						
Prayer						

TABLE 1 Offense analysis sheet

Complete this evaluation for each situation that seems to be a great challenge. This might help in situations where you just cannot identify why someone reacts to you in an inappropriate way and you are determined to correct the relationship and make it right as God would desire. It can also be beneficial if it is a situation with a difficult-to-identify solution. I would suggest this exercise be as private as possible because it is for the purpose of self-improvement. However, this could lead to a conversation to further assist others or the offender should there be sincere reconciliation.

For resolution of a particular situation, sometimes a conversation can help to highlight aspects or factors that may otherwise be overlooked so that now they may be uncovered. Alternative solutions or outlooks may also provide a better understanding of choices available or opportunity for resolve.

> Where no counsel is, the people fall: but in the multitude
> of counsellors there is safety. (Proverbs 11:14)

Bearing this in mind, you should know that confident, mature guidance is most important. Additionally, with such input, careful analysis is important prior to any conclusive decision-making. Be slow to speak.

> Why, my beloved brothers, let every man be swift to hear,
> slow to speak, slow to wrath. (James 1:19)

Perhaps there are some generational issues that may be uncovered in your life. Be sure not to disregard the findings, but treat them as clues or leads to assist you in arriving at a targeted solution. It is always better to be well-informed.

Release the Offender

Now that you know a reasonable amount about your challenge, it is important to use the analysis to better inform intended actions. As the Lord's Prayer suggests, we must forgive in order to be forgiven; we must now release all offenders. The act of forgiving involves more than just saying, "I forgive you." It incorporates some actions also, as follows:

1. Eliminate emotional responses to hurt or disappointment (any resulting emotion). This must be done.
2. Give a pardon for all areas of offense.
3. Display God's love.

Release the Offense and the Offender by Way of
Thought and Emotions. Give Relief from Hurt, Remove
Obligations, and Show Sympathy. Expect Nothing

Oftentimes I hear stories of people who committed a crime because they were angry, or because they felt rejected sometime in the past when someone did something to them or some experience crippled them or maybe destroyed what they valued. To be victorious, truly victorious, we must always be prepared to shed excessive opinions, conduct, and words. These occupy areas where valuable destiny-shaping and caring commodity can thrive.

> Why seeing we also are compassed about with so great a
> cloud of witnesses, let us lay aside every weight, and the sin
> which does so easily beset us, and let us run with patience
> the race that is set before us. (Hebrews 12:1)

Emotions, opinions, actions, people, and things can all be considered burdens when they fail to inspire us to reach our goal.

> Recompense to no man evil for evil. Provide things honest
> in the sight of all men. If it be possible, as much as lies in
> you, live peaceably with all men.

> Dearly beloved, avenge not yourselves, but rather give
> place to wrath: for it is written, Vengeance is mine; I will
> repay, said the Lord. Therefore if your enemy hunger, feed
> him; if he thirst, give him drink: for in so doing you shall
> heap coals of fire on his head. Be not overcome of evil, but
> overcome evil with good. (Romans 12:17–21)

Walk in Love

> And walk in love, as Christ also has loved us, and has given himself for us an offering and a sacrifice to God for a sweet smelling smell.
>
> —Ephesians 5:2

As believers, we are identified by the love of Christ. We are recognized as Christians because others are able to see Christ Jesus in us. We need each other. The design of God's body, being the church, is a clear picture of the manner in which He expects His creation to interact. God's love has no reservations or limits. Everyone is on the same playing field with God. Love has no prejudices and affords equal opportunities and unbiased treatment or response. Love will not highlight faults but will seek to assist brothers and sisters in the faith.

> Love works no ill to his neighbor: therefore love is the fulfilling of the law. (Romans 13:10)
>
> *Further reading:* 1 Corinthians 13

Seek Reconciliation

> And all things are of God, who has reconciled us to himself by Jesus Christ, and has given to us the ministry of reconciliation;
>
> To wit, that God was in Christ, reconciling the world to himself, not imputing their trespasses to them; and has committed to us the word of reconciliation.
>
> —2 Corinthians 5:18–19

Reconciliation is the first ministry we are called to. The Lord gave each believer this charge. While reconciliation would follow forgiveness, it takes time and is conditional. Trusting after an offense is a process, and this varies with individuals. The reconciliation process hinges on truthful confessions of and repentance from wrongdoings. The offender should accept his or her wrong and acknowledge the hurt caused. During this process there will be discussions about resolution and guidelines for reconciliation.

Free Your Mind and Heart from the Thought and Hurt of the Past

> Casting down imaginations, and every high thing that exalts itself against the knowledge of God, and bringing into captivity every thought to the obedience of Christ.

—2 Corinthians 10:5

It is a very difficult task to endeavor to live a consecrated life and continuously remember and feel the hurt associated with experiences you went through. This loop of thought and painful emotions is a weight, and with each time the thought process occurs, it contaminates the heart and mind. The impression of forgiveness may even be eliminated, and unforgiveness will spring up again. It is helpful and most recommended to deny yourself the opportunity to accumulate these thoughts as they encourage not only unforgiveness but also self-pity and may even motivate acts of vengeance, spite, and bitterness.

An excellent way to look at your situation is to remember that you need to accommodate and nourish thoughts of God's grace and healing for your health and well-being. To achieve wholeness, you must place considerable attention on your process of healing of a past hurt, not on the hurtful acts themselves. Those latter acts you would have presented already in prayer when you forgave those persons who offended you. It is important to move forward by refusing to relive the pain and the experience through mental images and emotions. This will allow you more time and effort for making your victory a reality.

*   *   *

Prayer

Father, in Your name, I confess every act of unforgiveness right now, and I forgive those who have wronged me. I ask You to forgive me and cleanse me from all sinful emotions of the heart (hate, bitterness, malice, guile, etc.). As I forgive others, may those I have offended also forgive me.

Create in me a clean heart, and renew a right spirit within me.

In Jesus's name, amen.

Declaration

I release everyone who has offended me.

I release myself from guilt and the bondage of unforgiveness. I will not be a willful prisoner to any sin of the heart. I treasure Christ; He holds my heart. I declare that those who have offended me are not obligated to, nor am I requiring that they, satisfy any loss resulting from the offense at any time. I release them in the name of Jesus.

CHAPTER 5
Think Only on the Word of God

This book of the law shall not depart out of your mouth; but you shall meditate therein day and night, that you may observe to do according to all that is written therein: for then you shall make your way prosperous, and then you shall have good success.

—Joshua 1:8

It is impossible for a giraffe to live a healthy and prolonged life if it eats meat instead of the vegetation it is designed to consume. Likewise, a believer lives by the very Word of God.

> But he answered and said, It is written, Man shall not live by bread alone, but by every word that proceeds out of the mouth of God. (Matthew 4:4)

Every part of our being is nurtured spiritually by the scriptures. Hearing is not sufficient. The spoken Word must be internalized by the hearer. This occurs through study, memorization, and meditation. We know that the scripture states that which we think established who we are.

> For as he thinks in his heart, so is he: Eat and drink, said he to you; but his heart is not with you. (Proverbs 23:7)

Our spiritual well-being, and ultimately our physical existence, depends heavily upon our commitment to know the Word of God. We must be familiar, by studying, and seek to find God's truth in every challenge. When scriptures are found, read each, study them, and quote them regularly. This is the feeding process. This fortifies believers in the time of trouble. They become well aware of God's thoughts concerning their circumstances, and the Holy Spirit brings all scripture to their remembrance.

> But the Comforter, which is the Holy Ghost, whom the Father will send in my name, he shall teach you all things, and bring all things to your remembrance, whatever I have said to you. (John 14:26)

> My son, attend to my words; incline your ear to my sayings.

> Let them not depart from your eyes; keep them in the middle of your heart.

For they are life to those that find them, and health to all their flesh. (Proverbs 4:20–22)

He taught me also, and said to me, Let your heart retain my words: keep my commandments, and live. (Proverbs 4:4)

Release the Word of God Concerning Your Situation

Death and life are in the power of the tongue: and they that love it shall eat the fruit thereof.

—Proverbs 18:21

While we understand that the ideal resolution of any situation is the will of God, in fighting for our breakthrough, we are encouraged to release the Word of God concerning the challenge. Any other solution may create further challenges. To release simply suggests to speak and believe the Word simultaneously in every challenge. The process is simple.

I will give you an example of this in my life. Some years ago, I experienced severe attack in multiple areas of my life at the same time. Looking back, I know it was God who brought me out and most definitely only God who gave me the power to escape victoriously. It seemed impossible for me to escape total destruction. The people in my immediate circle were trying to convince me that I was doomed. But I believed God. Financially, I had nothing. There was one thing happening for me: God loved me. People seemed to conveniently know when and where I would show up and tried to avoid me. I felt I was, and I actually was, despised and rejected. I found it difficult to confide in a believer to ask for prayers because they all knew my plight and had already sentenced me. But this hurt but did not move me. I believed God. Heavy, discouraged, depressed, and depressed, but still full of hope in God, I cried out to the Lord.

I used this principle of speaking the Word. The Word I spoke by faith as I looked into my despair and dark, most certain doom was taken from Psalm 1. I will never forget this. It was in response to someone who should have been fighting with me laughing and condemning me instead; broken, weak, frail, and hurting, but believing God, I exclaimed, "Goodness and mercy shall follow hard after me!"

At that very moment I was able to stand. My spirit was strengthened. Hope superseded what I knew. These words were spoken in the strongest of confidence—confidence not in myself or my situation but in God. The truth is even that I agreed I was in a horrible mess. This confession gave me the push to expect God to honor His Word. Sometime into my fight, God placed a beautiful quotation into my spirit, and it is now my life statement appended to my emails. It states, "Consented impossibilities become reality when driven by the catalyst of passion."

> Then said the Lord to me, You have well seen: for I will hasten my word to perform it. (Jeremiah 1:12)

I was not disappointed, and through it all I was not put to shame. God in His time delivered me from all my troubles. Praise God. As Jeremiah documented, He can certainly move the victory into reality quickly.

Confession is a powerful initiative in victory. You usually receive what you believe or confess. By stating God's Word, you eliminate every conflicting opinion and plan for you that resists God's will.

> For by your words you shall be justified, and by your words you shall be condemned. (Matthew 12:37)

> For the word of God is quick, and powerful, and sharper than any two edged sword, piercing even to the dividing asunder of soul and spirit, and of the joints and marrow, and is a discerner of the thoughts and intents of the heart. (Hebrews 4:12)

> All scripture is given by inspiration of God, and is profitable for doctrine, for reproof, for correction, for instruction in righteousness:

> That the man of God may be perfect, thoroughly furnished to all good works. (2 Timothy 3:16–17)

Quote and Memorize the Word Specific to Your Situation

The table below provides suggested scriptures based on identified situations for the reader to read, memorize and quote daily or in prayer.

Situation	Scripture
Pain	Romans 8:18 For I reckon that the sufferings of this present time are not worthy to be compared with the glory which shall be revealed in us.
Hurt	Psalm 34:18 The Lord is near to them that are of a broken heart; and saves such as be of a contrite spirit
Strife	Romans 14:19 Let us therefore follow after the things which make for peace, and things with which one may edify another.
Fear	Isaiah 41:10 Fear you not; for I am with you: be not dismayed; for I am your God: I will strengthen you; yes, I will help you; yes, I will uphold you with the right hand of my righteousness.
Failure	Psalm 73:26 My flesh and my heart fails: but God is the strength of my heart, and my portion for ever.
Rejection	Luke 10:16 He that hears you hears me; and he that despises you despises me; and he that despises me despises him that sent me.
Defeat	Ephesians 6:10–11 Finally, my brothers, be strong in the Lord, and in the power of his might. Put on the whole armor of God, that you may be able to stand against the wiles of the devil.

Situation	Scripture
Betrayal	Psalm 1:1 Blessed is the man that walks not in the counsel of the ungodly, nor stands in the way of sinners, nor sits in the seat of the scornful.
Mind battles	James 1:8 A double minded man [is] unstable in all his ways.
Sexual impurities	1 Corinthians 6:18 Flee fornication. Every sin that a man does is without the body; but he that commits fornication sins against his own body.
Family	Ephesians 5:21 Submitting yourselves one to another in the fear of God.
Friendship	Proverbs 18:24 A man that has friends must show himself friendly: and there is a friend that sticks closer than a brother. A man [that hath] friends must shew himself friendly: and there is a friend [that] sticketh closer than a brother.
Love	1 John 4:7 Beloved, let us love one another: for love is of God; and every one that loves is born of God, and knows God.
Divorce	Matthew 19:6 Why they are no more two, but one flesh. What therefore God has joined together, let not man put asunder.
Work	James 1:25 But whoever looks into the perfect law of liberty, and continues therein, he being not a forgetful hearer, but a doer of the work, this man shall be blessed in his deed.
Education	Proverbs 16:16 How much better is it to get wisdom than gold! and to get understanding rather to be chosen than silver!

Situation	Scripture
Hardship	2 Timothy 2:3–5 You therefore endure hardness, as a good soldier of Jesus Christ.
Stagnation	Zephaniah 1:12 And it shall come to pass at that time, that I will search Jerusalem with candles, and punish the men that are settled on their lees: that say in their heart, The Lord will not do good, neither will he do evil.
Procrastination	Proverbs 15:19 The way of the slothful man is as an hedge of thorns: but the way of the righteous is made plain.

Accept and Desire Nothing but the Perfect Will of the Lord

I cannot emphasize enough how important it is to study and memorize the Word of God. When you know what God says in His Word regarding your challenge, you will see the open door to get out. He is the door. This door reveals His perfect will. It will be seen only through the mirror of the Word. A desperate person will search without fail for food. Food is a source of sustenance. The Word is our life. It delivers not only from trouble but also from the power of sin.

> And be not conformed to this world: but be you transformed by the renewing of your mind, that you may prove what is that good, and acceptable, and perfect, will of God. (Romans 12:2)

Jeremiah obviously had some degree of problems when he wrote the verse that follows. His heart seems to have led him on a quest for God's Word. He writes how he found God's Word and speaks of its refreshing nature. When we arrive to the place where our mind is in complete agreement with the Word of God, we will experience supernatural transformation in our conduct, lifestyle, and battles. We will grow into victory. Jeremiah concluded that he had a transformation because of the fact that he belonged to God.

> Your words were found, and I did eat them; and your word was to me the joy and rejoicing of my heart: for I am called by your name, O Lord God of hosts. (Jeremiah 15:16)

*   *   *

Prayer

Father, in the name of Jesus, I acknowledge that I am not where You want me to be. I accept the fact that my thoughts are not Your thoughts; my mind is not in alignment with Your Word. I ask Your forgiveness and that You would uproot every thought, opinion, and imagination that is not of You. Father, Your Spirit renews my mind as I meditate on Your Word. Let me think like You. I cast down every imagination and everything that exalts itself above the knowledge of Christ. I am Yours, Father. Your Word gives light and inspired victorious solutions. I praise You now for Your light and the power of Your Word.

In Jesus's mighty name, amen.

Declaration

Right now, in the name of Jesus, I take authority over every one of my thoughts. I command right now that they be subject to and influenced by the Word of God. I bring every one of my thoughts into captivity. I cast down imagination and every high thing that exalts itself against the knowledge of Christ. I eat the Word and command it to be like fire in my life, in my mouth. As I release the Word of God, I command that it returns to me, having completed what it was sent to do.

I command my mind to line up with the Word of God. I command my heart, my spirit, my soul, and my body to respond only to the Word of God. I accept nothing less in the name of Jesus.

CHAPTER 6
Know the Will of God Concerning You

Paul, an apostle of Jesus Christ by the will of God.

—2 Corinthians 1:1

Determine as you read *Release the Overcomer's Anointing* that you will assume your rightful status as a student of the Word, an understudy of Christ. Too many perish for lack of wisdom. The body of Christ does not know the Word of God. It is an estranged text. The Bible has every instruction for us to successfully carry out our lives; we just need to become acquainted with the pages and "let them become one with us."

Let's have a look at how the word is advises in science, communication and conflict resolution:

o **Examples Where the Word of God May Be Used in Science**

The fear of the Lord is the beginning of knowledge: but fools despise wisdom and instruction. (Proverbs 1:7)

O Timothy, keep that which is committed to your trust, avoiding profane and vain babblings, and oppositions of science falsely so called. (1 Timothy 6:20)

And God said, Let the earth bring forth the living creature after his kind, cattle, and creeping thing, and beast of the earth after his kind: and it was so. (Genesis 1:24)

A merry heart does good like a medicine: but a broken spirit dries the bones. (Proverbs 17:22 KJV)

o **History, Rise and Fall of Nations, Multiple Languages**

And the whole earth was of one language, and of one speech.

And it came to pass, as they journeyed from the east, that they found a plain in the land of Shinar; and they dwelled there.

And they said one to another, Go to, let us make brick, and burn them thoroughly. And they had brick for stone, and slime had they for mortar.

And they said, Go to, let us build us a city and a tower, whose top may reach to heaven; and let us make us a name, lest we be scattered abroad on the face of the whole earth.

And the Lord came down to see the city and the tower, which the children of men built.

And the Lord said, Behold, the people is one, and they have all one language; and this they begin to do: and now nothing will be restrained from them, which they have imagined to do.

Go to, let us go down, and there confound their language, that they may not understand one another's speech.

So the Lord scattered them abroad from there on the face of all the earth: and they left off to build the city.

Therefore is the name of it called Babel; because the Lord did there confound the language of all the earth: and from there did the Lord scatter them abroad on the face of all the earth. (Genesis 11:1–9)

And God said, Behold, I have given you every herb bearing seed, which is on the face of all the earth, and every tree, in the which is the fruit of a tree yielding seed; to you it shall be for meat.

And to every beast of the earth, and to every fowl of the air, and to every thing that creeps on the earth, wherein there is life, I have given every green herb for meat: and it was so.

And God saw every thing that he had made, and, behold, it was very good. And the evening and the morning were the sixth day. (Genesis 1:29–31)

Drink no longer water, but use a little wine for your stomach's sake and your often infirmities. (1 Timothy 5:23)

Take you also to you wheat, and barley, and beans, and lentils, and millet, and fitches, and put them in one vessel, and make you bread thereof, according to the number of the days that you shall lie on your side, three hundred and ninety days shall you eat thereof. (Ezekiel 4:9 KJV)

o **Conflict Resolution**

Do all things without murmurings and disputings. (Philippians 2:14)

And Eliud begat Eleazar; and Eleazar begat Matthan; and Matthan begat Jacob. (Matthew 18:15)

Be you angry, and sin not: let not the sun go down on your wrath. (Ephesians 4:26)

And some days after Paul said to Barnabas, Let us go again and visit our brothers in every city where we have preached the word of the Lord, and see how they do.

And Barnabas determined to take with them John, whose surname was Mark.

But Paul thought not good to take him with them, who departed from them from Pamphylia, and went not with them to the work.

And the contention was so sharp between them, that they departed asunder one from the other: and so Barnabas took Mark, and sailed to Cyprus;

And Paul chose Silas, and departed, being recommended by the brothers to the grace of God.

And he went through Syria and Cilicia, confirming the churches. (Acts 15:36–41)

When we become passionate about a particular thing, perhaps this is a good place to begin. God places good desires in our hearts. Following these will lead us to an understanding of His plan for us. The foregoing suggestion is a good response to writing a clear course of action to follow our passion. We should seek scriptural references. These may confirm whether it is a concept from God or not. Once we confirm, a quick surf on the internet may show us examples or inspire us to begin the process of walking in divine order.

The moving of God can be compared to a time bomb placed in the midst of the enemy's plans. At His good pleasure alone, He completely obliterates the opposing assignments, strategies, networks, organizations, and hierarchies, overthrowing, dislodging, and annihilating high places and those who conspire in the regiments of darkness. We may ask the question in our situation "Can God?"

The answer always is, "But that's just God!" All glory!

Know Who You Are in God

> And such as do wickedly against the covenant shall he corrupt by flatteries: but the people that do know their God shall be strong, and do exploits.

> —Daniel 11:32

When individuals are aware and confident of their identities, they will not be easily convinced to act or think out of character. To have self-awareness and confidence is a sign of maturity. Mature believers do not have to respond or perform to please an audience. They do not need the validation of others. They may welcome the encouragement but will not be manipulated by it. Identifying with Christ means we are grafted into His body.

> And they also, if they abide not still in unbelief, shall be grafted in: for God is able to graft them in again. (Romans 11:23)

We are hidden with Christ in God.

> For you are dead, and your life is hid with Christ in God.
> (Colossians 3:3)

When you are seen, God is seen in you.

> I am crucified with Christ: nevertheless I live; yet not I,
> but Christ lives in me: and the life which I now live in the
> flesh I live by the faith of the Son of God, who loved me,
> and gave himself for me. (Galatians 2:20)

After researching the scriptures in previous chapters, you should be comfortable now with your identity in Christ Jesus. Understanding and applying what you have learned will bring you into a place of dominance and spiritual authority.

> Being confident of this very thing, that he which hath
> begun a good work in you will perform it until the day of
> Jesus Christ. (Philippians 1:6)

As believers, we know that we are ambassadors, appointed by God Himself. We have all liberty yet abstain from many things for His glory so that we may be above reproach. Paul made his position known:

> Yes doubtless, and I count all things but loss for the
> excellency of the knowledge of Christ Jesus my Lord: for
> whom I have suffered the loss of all things, and do count
> them but dung, that I may win Christ. (Philippians 3:8)

Do not consider this a loss or misfortune as contemporary society may think. I maintain that loss or change for God's glory is an honor. So, judgment or criticism will not be intimidating either. This sacrifice brings us into a covenant relationship with the God who is Lord of all. We then are confident and assured of His love; therefore, we live with this persuasion.

If we suffer, we shall also reign with him: if we deny him,
he also will deny us. (2 Timothy 2:12)

You must know your purpose and work it. Let your faith become
one with God's Word. Know and speak the Word of God regarding your
situation. Hold on to God's promises and remain consistent. Realize where
you are as you evaluate your position. Weather the storms of criticism,
hardship, and rejection; God makes the rejected to become the chief
cornerstone.

Know That He Wants the Best for You

For I know the thoughts that I think toward you, said the
Lord, thoughts of peace, and not of evil, to give you an
expected end.

—Jeremiah 29:11

This world was designed with humankind at the heart of it. We were
formed in the image of God. We look like Him. He shares Himself with
us. We are partakers of His grace. We are joint heirs with Christ. We
did absolutely nothing to acquire such favor. God, desiring a people who
would bear His image, sacrificed everything, His Son, for us. This act of
redemption is a powerful statement, one that is discussed across religions.

Beloved, I wish above all things that you may prosper and
be in health, even as your soul prospers. (3 John 1:2)

I had a conversation with an Indian friend of mine in which she
marveled at the thought of this God who answers prayers, who heals, who
delivers, and who blesses. Her response to me after I had related event after
event where I had seen God heal people who were afflicted with illnesses
was astonishing. I continued to tell her of how I prayed and believed God
for a job in a specific area and He delivered. Her response was, "Krishna
has never answered me. Wow, Darnell, I have to read the Bible."

I believe this is what distinguishes our faith. We have a God who cares for His people. He wants to share everything He has with us.

> Fear not, little flock; for it is your Father's good pleasure
> to give you the kingdom. (Luke 12:32)

Paul expressed the heart of God when he said, "Beloved, I wish above all things that thou mayest prosper and be in health, even as thy soul prospereth" (3 John 1:2).

Everything we have, all we hope for or can ever attain, comes from God. He imparts to us continuously. Oftentimes we may not see or be sensitive to the opportunities that present themselves as a result of fellowship with God. It is imperative that we be alert at all times. Few things will just slip through our hands. Consider each day as a gift. Live it with joy and excitement. To be alive in Christ is a great privilege.

Life in Christ is designed for the believer to prosper in every area of his or her life. If we listen intently to God's directives, He will lead us into green pastures. The Word of God is our guide; millions before us have experienced the truth in the scriptures becoming reality in their lives from generation to generation. The Word has not changed and will never change.

> Jesus Christ the same yesterday, and to day, and for ever.
> (Hebrews 13:8)

*   *   *

Prayer

> Father, I have not walked before You in my true identity. I ask Your pardon. Help me to see You in me, and give me the awareness of my existence in Your body. Cause me to see that I am not my own but that I was created for a divine purpose. Empower me to live in Your will and to walk in the authority entrusted to me by my spiritual

birthright. Thank You for the new birth and the status of royalty.

Amen.

Declaration

Now with the knowledge gained through Your Word, I step into position and acknowledge that I am Christ's and He is mine. I embrace the fact that I look like You, my thoughts are influenced by Your Word, my heart is transformed, and my words flow from my heart's content, which is now and always will be Your Word. I command right now that I not be deceived by the devices of the enemy. The wisdom of God contained in the Word will illuminate my path. It has illuminated all doubt, and right now I am confident and know that I am a joint heir with Christ and possess the keys to the kingdom of God. I am aware that the King of Glory lives in me. I live like it, speak like it, work like it, praise like it, and pray like it.

Hallelujah!

CHAPTER 7
Let No One Condemn You

Who is he that condemns? It is Christ that died, yes rather, that is risen again, who is even at the right hand of God, who also makes intercession for us.

—Romans 8:34

Jesus Christ Is Our Advocate

> For there is one God, and one mediator between God and men, the man Christ Jesus.

> —1 Timothy 2:5

As the scripture states, humankind is not even in the equation to hear from or receive from God. Wow! All the teachings we have been adhering to make us believe that there must be this man or woman of God who is appointed to pray on our behalf so that we might have an oracle. I think that this teaching has been successful in the church because believers do not know their own authority or rather have opted not to make the sacrifice to become intimate with God, preferring that others make that sacrifice on their behalf. This is not God's preference. But the scripture clearly states that the person called Jesus is this Mediator. He is the One who was crucified for the cleansing of our sins. We can ask people to agree with us as the apostles agreed with Jesus, but we can feel confident to pray and know that God will hear us and answer us. Jesus, not humankind, is always interceding for us at the right hand of God.

Humankind cannot condemn spiritually simply because we do not have the power to pardon sin. This alone belongs to Jesus.

> Who is he that condemns? It is Christ that died, yes rather, that is risen again, who is even at the right hand of God, who also makes intercession for us. (Romans 8:34)

He solely took on the power of darkness on Calvary's cross. Even the Father did not bear the burden of sin that beautiful day. Jesus and Jesus alone bore it.

> But God commends his love toward us, in that, while we were yet sinners, Christ died for us. (Romans 5:8)

He was appointed by God to redeem us from the curse of sin. God sees the blood of His Son each time we sin.

What shall we say then? Shall we continue in sin, that grace may abound? God forbid. How shall we, that are dead to sin, live any longer therein? (Romans 6:2)

While we understand that sin should never be our practice, we also know that in Christ we have pardon for repented sin.

If we confess our sins, he is faithful and just to forgive us our sins, and to cleanse us from all unrighteousness. (1 John 1:9)

This is a personal exchange. There is no mediator. We go directly to God, and He communicates directly with us. The elimination of a mediator because of Christ's sacrifice gives us full access to grace.

Let us therefore come boldly to the throne of grace, that we may obtain mercy, and find grace to help in time of need. (Hebrews 4:16)

The opinion of a trusted friend or our greatest enemy does not influence God's pardon. Once we confess our sins, He will honor His Word and forgive us. We do not have to continue with a guilty conscience. Once we sincerely confess and turn away from sin, we are free. This is the promise in the shedding of the precious blood of Jesus. Who can challenge this?

Only God knows the heart of humankind.

I the Lord search the heart, I try the reins, even to give every man according to his ways, and according to the fruit of his doings. (Jeremiah 17:10)

We see the mistakes and the efforts, but the motive behind all this is seen by the One who created the organs and the human. He interprets meaning of the movements and the mode of operation of humankind. Humankind has many faces, portrayed to create an image in society, but God sees through all this.

The heart is deceitful above all things, and desperately wicked: who can know it? (Jeremiah 17:9)

We must be confident in the promises of the Word. Study it and apply it daily. Again, I state that it is our life. If God liberates us, not even the clergyman with the highest position on earth can condemn us, not with his earthly authority and not with his doctrine or status.

If the Son therefore shall make you free, you shall be free indeed. (John 8:36)

Stand fast therefore in the liberty with which Christ has made us free, and be not entangled again with the yoke of bondage. (Galatians 5:1)

After communication, our challenge is to walk firmly in the forgiveness Christ gives. Being free from sin dismisses the curses that once attached themselves to us. We must understand that now blessings will follow us. Daily our expectancy should be in Christ's promises to us. The snare of sin condemns us, but the justification of Christ removes every burden.

Hear therefore, O Israel, and observe to do it; that it may be well with you, and that you may increase mightily, as the Lord God of your fathers has promised you, in the land that flows with milk and honey. (Deuteronomy 6:3)

There is therefore now no condemnation to them which are in Christ Jesus, who walk not after the flesh, but after the Spirit. For the law of the Spirit of life in Christ Jesus has made me free from the law of sin and death. (Romans 8:1)

God seeks to give everyone who confesses a new beginning. He completely erases the sin prior to our confession. While we may have some challenges because of our past choices, God gives us wisdom to overcome these. Even in going through this corrective stage, we are free. Sin makes us feel justified in continuing as usual, but the liberty of grace opens our eyes to God's truth and love.

> And that you put on the new man, which after God is created in righteousness and true holiness. (Ephesians 4:24)

Mention Your Past Only to Give God Glory

> Circumcised the eighth day, of the stock of Israel, of the tribe of Benjamin, an Hebrew of the Hebrews; as touching the law, a Pharisee.
>
> —Philippians 3:5

Paul was not always a believer. For years he persecuted the Christian church. He was known for his violence against the early church. Upon his conversion, the Lord changed his outlook. Yes, he temporarily lost his sight. But in the process, there was a transformation. The Christ of the early church communicated with Paul in power. This mighty man was dominated by just the appearance of the King of kings. He bowed in submission, and the King of Glory entered his life.

Christ erased the past conduct of this Saul, a Roman soldier, and gave him a new image. He made him to look like Him. He changed the goals of this man. Now, instead of fighting against the church of God, Paul fought with the body of Christ and took a leading role.

Most importantly, God changed his name. The early Romans believed that knowing the name of Rome would give their enemies power to conquer them. So, the citizens referred to this great nation as Rome, but the true name was never known. Rome was a domineering country for centuries. Saul, the Roman centurion, now because of an encounter with the Lord, mighty in battle, became Paul, apostle of the Lord Jesus Christ. He conducted himself accordingly.

So, you might recall, the early church was afraid of Paul. They knew of his past acts. However, they were told to accept Paul into their fellowship because of the Lord's purpose. Paul experienced great opposition and persecution, but he lived an exemplary life in Christ. God had justified him and erased his past. So, Paul left it there.

There was a mention of his past, though, but he mentioned this to affirm his position in Christ. He did not boast about how evil he used to be or how much he had gotten away with; instead, he honored God.

> Though I might also have confidence in the flesh. If any other man thinks that he has whereof he might trust in the flesh, I more:
>
> Circumcised the eighth day, of the stock of Israel, of the tribe of Benjamin, an Hebrew of the Hebrews; as touching the law, a Pharisee;
>
> Concerning zeal, persecuting the church; touching the righteousness which is in the law, blameless.
>
> But what things were gain to me, those I counted loss for Christ.
>
> Yes doubtless, and I count all things but loss for the excellency of the knowledge of Christ Jesus my Lord: for whom I have suffered the loss of all things, and do count them but dung, that I may win Christ. (Philippians 3:4–8)

* * *

Prayer

> Father, I acknowledge You as my Savior, and I thank You for Your blood, which cleanses me of every sin. Allow my mind to embrace the truth that You have canceled the power of sin and there is now no condemnation of me as I

walk in Your Word. Receive all glory from my life, Father, as I walk in the new life through Jesus, Your Son.

Amen.

Declaration

I release all guilt of past failures; I release the opinion of humankind; and I cleave to the liberty in Christ because it is what has made me free. I refuse to be entangled with the bondage of sin on account of personal opinion or the response of others. I hide myself in Your Word. I will continually walk in the power of Your Word, free from the chains of the past. Everything I do will give You glory. I plunge under the blood of Jesus, my refuge. I declare that I am free indeed.

CHAPTER 8
Wait Patiently

Wait on the Lord: be of good courage, and he shall strengthen your heart: wait, I say, on the Lord.

—Psalm 27:14

God has time and opportunity aligned in your favor. He has given every believer all the resources needed to live a fulfilling and successful life. Time, however, reveals God's plan. Unfortunately, time does not adjust in response to our haste or desperation but acts according to God's perfect will. God cares for us. He knows that we are in trouble. Sometimes He allows us to go through challenges, but He ministers to us each step of the way. He may deliberately shield us from going through other circumstances. God is the author of our faith. He knows every detail of every day, past, present, and future. He understands the conflicts and knows the route we are taking to get out. In His plan, our efforts must conform to His Word. We are to trust Him without doubt.

Many times, we only complicate things with our premature responses. Yes, it is natural to desire a speedy exit from every opposition. Many times, such opposition, though painful and hard, is designed for our good. Even in our trials, God gets glory. The important point to establish here is that each experience is for spiritual growth and maturity. Going through life's processes is itself a process of enlightenment. It is important to remain in these for the time God has appointed. We need to be careful to note lessons taught and to learn well. These lessons serve to reinforce the power of Christ in our lives and reveal His love to us. We develop a profound intimate relationship with God. We hear His voice more clearly. We also understand His will better after coming out richer.

This understanding of the beauty of trials helped me to think much differently about them. Of course, I don't advertise "Trouble wanted here!" No. As long as we live, we will have struggles. So, I know they do show up now and then, sometimes pretty often. When they do reveal themselves, I look at them to see where God wants to take me. I realize that if He is taking me to a closer walk with Him, consequent to successfully overcoming, it is for my good. This permission that He gives for the storm to form is for me to see even more of Him. It is all in love.

The reality is that God always plans for our success. Challenges paint a deceitful picture.

> And we know that all things work together for good to
> them that love God, to them who are the called according
> to his purpose. (Romans 8:28)

We simply need to observe the indications in the Word and follow them, every instruction and inspiration. God is faithful, and His plan supersedes those in opposition to it. Further, to tempt or afflict any born-again believer, Satan must go to the Lord and ask His permission. He cannot target a believer without cause or without permission from God. This same God has designed life for us to overcome. So, you see, everything is for our good.

> Now there was a day when the sons of God came to present themselves before the Lord, and Satan came also among them. (Job 1:6)

Read this chapter(Job 1) for further understanding.

Abraham Waited for a Son

> And I will make my covenant between me and you, and will multiply you exceedingly.
>
> —Genesis 17:2

At the time of this promise, according to the scripture, Abram was ninety-nine years old.

> And when Abram was ninety years old and nine, the Lord appeared to Abram, and said to him, I am the Almighty God; walk before me, and be you perfect. (Genesis 17:1)

The possibility of someone his age fathering a child seems to us to be nonexistent. However, with God, all things are possible (Matthew 19:26). Abram waited for some time even after this promise was made before he was able to see its fulfillment. God spoke to Abraham and told him that in spite of Sarah's age, she would give him a son and his name would be called Isaac. Abraham, as God had renamed him, was to be the father of many nations. Sarah heard the conversation, and in her unbelief, she laughed. She also denied such a response to what she had heard when asked by Abraham. This unbelief did not prevent God's blessing, because Abraham believed God and the covenant was not with Sarah really, even though she was to be the natural mother of the child.

Abraham, in an effort to speed up the process, fathered a child with Sarah's slave. This created a problem that still exists today. The slave's child, being Abraham's firstborn, naturally may have felt a right to an inheritance from his father. Isaac, the child in marriage, got everything. They both influenced the growth of a nation—and today Iraq and Iran remain at war. However, the Lord told Abraham during their initial conversation that He had made the covenant with Isaac.

Process Is a Part of the Union

Years ago, the Lord showed me a dream that, to me, had a very powerful message. I had been asking Him to use me and purify me for His work. I believe this was His way of showing me what He would do to fulfill my request. He placed me in a furnace. I was being turned on a metal pole. I knew it was me, but the female figure was not of flesh. It was made of gold. This gold figure was going through the refiner's process. I knew that He was showing me that I would have to go through a process of refinement and sanctification.

God gets glory out of our lives whether we go through trials or experience peace and comfort. However, trials are designed to expedite the process of union with God. They bring us to a place of authority and honor in the kingdom of God.

> If we suffer, we shall also reign with him: if we deny him, he also will deny us. (2 Timothy 2:12)

Accept God's Peace

> And let the peace of God rule in your hearts, to the which also you are called in one body; and be you thankful.
>
> —Colossians 3:15

It can prove to be very difficult to hear God's voice if one's spirit is in turmoil. Peace suggests a level of confidence and strong belief in God's ability to deliver. It is a confirmation of faith in God. The peace that God gives will never be understood by humankind totally, simply because there is no explanation for people to smile and encourage or even give to another individual if their homes have been destroyed, if they've recently lost their jobs, or if they have few options remaining. Abraham waited twenty-five years. Hebrews verifies that he was confident and did not doubt.

> He staggered not at the promise of God through unbelief; but was strong in faith, giving glory to God;

> And being fully persuaded that, what he had promised, he was able also to perform.

> And therefore it was imputed to him for righteousness.

> Therefore being justified by faith, we have peace with God through our Lord Jesus Christ: ...

> By whom also we have access by faith into this grace wherein we stand, and rejoice in hope of the glory of God. (Romans 4:20–22; 5:2)

When we present our petitions to the Lord, He responds to us. Remember, He has a plan for our lives, and in asking His intervention, we are asking Him to implement His divine order. Depending on the damage we would have done, for His plan to bring about His order we may have to shed or accept some things.

He wants us to sleep well.

> It is vain for you to rise up early, to sit up late, to eat the bread of sorrows: for so he giveth his beloved sleep. (Psalm 127:2)

We should become comfortable after we would have made our request known to Him, understanding that He is in control of everything.

To affirm this, God extends His peace to us. Once we accept this, by understanding His Word, we will not fret.

> And the peace of God, which passes all understanding, shall keep your hearts and minds through Christ Jesus. (Philippians 4:7)

The Peace of God
The peace of God does or is the following things:

- Rules the heart of humankind
- Is an instrument God uses in sanctification
- Preserves the spirit, soul, and body
- Causes us to sleep contentedly
- Keeps our hearts and minds
- Is above all knowledge bases
- Allows us to stand before God
- Causes us to rejoice.

Persevere

> Why take to you the whole armor of God, that you may be able to withstand in the evil day, and having done all, to stand.
>
> —Ephesians 6:13

Weather the storm, criticisms, and hardships. God makes the rejected to become the chief cornerstone. Challenges do not cease to exist just because we decide to do better or make things work. We must understand that as long as we live, we will have challenges. The difference between our circumstances and those of others is that Jesus, the Christ, is with us, sustaining us.

The scripture constantly teaches that nothing comes easy to the believer because he or she is not of this world. We are admonished to identify with Christ for this reason. We are also forewarned that we must fight for breakthrough, which will not come simply by naming and claiming alone. Sometimes this happens, but such is not always the case.

> You therefore endure hardness, as a good soldier of Jesus Christ.
>
> No man that wars entangles himself with the affairs of this life; that he may please him who has chosen him to be a soldier.
>
> And if a man also strive for masteries, yet is he not crowned, except he strive lawfully. (2 Timothy 2:3–5)

So, we must learn to allow the fruit of the Spirit to manifest in long-suffering and temperance. We must learn to search the scriptures and find the encouragement we need to give us the strength and hope we require to continue to push until we see the answers to our prayers. Always consider attitude.

Faith

> Now faith is the substance of things hoped for, the evidence of things not seen. For by it the elders obtained a good report.
>
> —Hebrews 11:1–3

Do you really wish to come out? Do you really want to be healed, to be set free, to draw near to God? If so, then my response to you is, "Have faith." Faith is more than just believing in something, trusting with all confidence. For the believer, faith is every Word from Genesis to Revelation. It is the spoken Word of God. It is the text; it is the system of beliefs. Our faith is what we believe and how we believe. It is both an expression and a thought. Faith is the Word, and the Word is Jesus.

For believers to have faith, their minds must ascend to the Word of God. Their minds and thoughts must be in agreement with God's Word.

This is why for Abraham, he felt he was justified by faith. Abraham believed very passionately until he came to live what he believed. He became one with what he believed as he lived and waited for the promise. He meditated on the Word of God and understood it. So, as he lived from day to day, he expected that promise to be fulfilled. He never doubted; rather he filled his mind with the hope that comes through faith.

> Through faith we understand that the worlds were framed by the word of God, so that things which are seen were not made of things which do appear. By faith Abel offered to God a more excellent sacrifice than Cain, by which he obtained witness that he was righteous, God testifying of his gifts: and by it he being dead yet speaks. By faith Enoch was translated that he should not see death; and was not found, because God had translated him: for before his translation he had this testimony, that he pleased God. But without faith it is impossible to please him: for he that comes to God must believe that he is, and that he is a rewarder of them that diligently seek him. By faith Noah, being warned of God of things not seen as yet, moved with fear, prepared an ark to the saving of his house; by which he condemned the world, and became heir of the righteousness which is by faith. By faith Abraham, when he was called to go out into a place which he should after receive for an inheritance, obeyed; and he went out, not knowing where he went. By faith he sojourned in the land of promise, as in a strange country, dwelling in tabernacles with Isaac and Jacob, the heirs with him of the same promise. (Hebrews 11:3–9)

I suggest that Hebrews 11 be read in its entirety and studied. It mentions so many good faith builders. This chapter establishes a case for faith outlook. The verified truth of Sarah's conception and healthy delivery of Isaac tells us that delay proves the might of God. Abraham is the father of many nations after so many years of waiting. This also affirms the faithfulness of God to honor His Word.

God is not a man, that he should lie; neither the son of man, that he should repent: has he said, and shall he not do it? or has he spoken, and shall he not make it good? (Numbers 23:19)

Some of the elders may not have experienced the promise of God in their lifetimes, but because they had internalized the promise, they had great confidence that God would fulfill His promise.

* * *

Prayer

Lord, teach me how to wait in You. Let the fruit of Your Spirit mature fully in me as I trust You through this. Allow me to see where You are taking me, and help me to note the lessons You would teach me well. Allow Your joy to fill me as I meditate on Your Word in the process of waiting for change. Give me faith as You did Abraham, who believed until he saw the promise You made—and as a result he was justified. I know that by faith I will live, so I rest in You, knowing that Your promises are sure. You are faithful and true, Father. Thank You for Your faithfulness to me.

In the name of Jesus, I pray.

Amen.

Declaration

I declare this day that the fruit of the spirit will be evident in me. I will walk in love, joy, peace, patience, kindness, goodness, faithfulness, gentleness, and self-control. I will not stagger at God's promises to me through unbelief, but I will continuously be strong and give all glory to God. I know that God is faithful and just and that He watches over His Word to perform it. So, I will trust, I will hope, I will praise, and I will work until He releases to me the grace I need. There is no failure in God, so I am encouraged and content.

I rest now in the comfort of the Word and declare that my season of change will come. It must come because of the promise Christ made.

Amen!

CHAPTER 9
Determine to Live Holy

Present your bodies a living sacrifice, holy, acceptable to
God, which is your reasonable service.

—Romans 12:1

Romans chapter twelve admonishes us to give our very beings to God, our Creator. Paul seeks to list the parts of the believer's existence to point out to readers and hearers alike that the process of submission is not partial but is a complete process. In obedience to God, surrendering to His will is a sacrifice. The nature of humankind is not total submission to God's Word but sin. In obedience to the call of God, Paul is admonishing believers to turn from sin completely, every part of us, and serve the Lord Jesus Christ.

> Why come out from among them, and be you separate, said the Lord, and touch not the unclean thing; and I will receive you. (2 Corinthians 6:17)

The life of a believer is one that is set apart. Paul said it like this:

> If a man therefore purge himself from these, he shall be a vessel to honor, sanctified, and meet for the master's use, and prepared to every good work. (2 Timothy 2:21)

We are expected to live a life of consecration. Holiness is a prized attribute of God. He admonishes the believer to be holy as He is holy. Without such care to cleanse ourselves from all unrighteousness, we will choose to distance ourselves from God. We must constantly remember to live according to our confession. Commitment to the tenets of Christianity demands a sincere allegiance. Compromise is unacceptable and will create a division between the Father and the individual. God will not accept the service of someone who is not true. This is what is called serving two masters. There must be a clear choice.

The presence of God sheds light on our shortcomings. So, each time we present ourselves in prayer, our sin will be uncovered. He will know without us saying. This is why He said at His appearance that those in sin would remain and those who have sanctified themselves will remain sanctified. His presence affirms our spiritual position.

> He that is unjust, let him be unjust still: and he which is filthy, let him be filthy still: and he that is righteous, let him be righteous still: and he that is holy, let him be holy still. (Revelation 22:11)

To fellowship with God in His approval, we must understand that the nature of God is holiness. And submitting to be like Him is the key to continued fellowship with God. To fellowship with God, there must be an acceptance of the nature of God. The individual must be in agreement with God.

Can two walk together, except they be agreed? (Amos 3:3)

Follow peace with all men, and holiness, without which no man shall see the Lord. (Hebrews 12:14)

Be True

Let us draw near with a true heart in full assurance of faith, having our hearts sprinkled from an evil conscience, and our bodies washed with pure water.

—Hebrews 10:22

Now therefore fear the Lord, and serve him in sincerity and in truth: and put away the gods which your fathers served on the other side of the flood, and in Egypt; and serve you the Lord.

And if it seem evil to you to serve the Lord, choose you this day whom you will serve; whether the gods which your fathers served that were on the other side of the flood, or the gods of the Amorites, in whose land you dwell: but as for me and my house, we will serve the Lord.

—Joshua 24:14–15

To be true suggests that we understand the requirements that God has for us and also that we are adhering to these wholeheartedly. To be true, we must remember that unless we are separate, we are compromised. That is, we are not in a position of divine surrender to only one God. It is impossible to serve two masters. God represents purity and truth. Any other God would be the opposite of this. It is impossible to be completely submitted to both light and darkness. It cannot work. God requires truth from the inner part of humankind.

> Behold, you desire truth in the inward parts: and in the hidden part you shall make me to know wisdom.
>
> Purge me with hyssop, and I shall be clean: wash me, and I shall be whiter than snow.
>
> Make me to hear joy and gladness; that the bones which you have broken may rejoice.
>
> Hide your face from my sins, and blot out all my iniquities.
>
> Create in me a clean heart, O God; and renew a right spirit within me.
>
> Cast me not away from your presence; and take not your holy spirit from me.
>
> Restore to me the joy of your salvation; and uphold me with your free spirit. (Psalm 51:6–12)

Everything we do should be with an effort to be pure before the Lord. We are expected to cleanse our hearts and serve God with our hearts, our souls, and all our strength.

> And thou shalt love the Lord thy God with all thy heart, and with all thy soul, and with thy entire mind, and with all thy strength: this is the first commandment. (Mark 12:30)

The true identity of a human being lies not in the physical body we see each day. The anatomy of an individual is designed to ensure that he or she is able to function here on earth. Jesus came to earth as a man to reach human beings. He came to complete the plan of redemption. Once He died on the cross, we were able to be forgiven and cleansed of righteousness.

So it is with humankind. We are in the world but not of the world because we were made in God's image and likeness. As Jesus took the form of a man and yet His Spirit existed, we are the same. We must look within the body. Our bodies house our spirits. There is no doubt that the body reacts and thinks, but so much more impacts these reactions or thoughts. The scripture speaks about the contents of a human being's heart.

This internal organ is a powerful tool and should be understood as such. The heart, according to the scripture, determines how spiritual we are. The thought and intent of the heart is revealed in our conversation and in what we do.

> For as he thinks in his heart, so is he: Eat and drink, said he to you; but his heart is not with you. (Proverbs 23:7)

We process thought and action based on the contents of our hearts. This is eminent when a conversation occurs. Listening carefully, one might hear the condition of the heart. The choice of words, the tone of voice, and the opinions expressed all tell whether the truth of God resides in an individual.

> O generation of vipers, how can you, being evil, speak good things? for out of the abundance of the heart the mouth speaks. (Matthew 12:34)

It is not the nature of someone who is not a Christian to speak the truth of Christ. Even in the most moral conversation, it will be obvious to a believer that the individual is not committed to true fellowship with Christ. The nature of the unbeliever is not righteousness but sin. Yes, it takes effort to remain separated, but if there is always a preference for sin, then there should be question marks. For a committed believer, there is always a passion and a thirst for more of Christ. This indicates truth. The more we realize how far from God we really are, the more we ask Him to draw us closer. We read His Word, live it, and pray it to Him. He expects a holy reverence of His name. This becomes easy when the truth is inside us.

Be Consistent

The blogger Abdol Rauf is noted for saying, "What is consistent in your life; is your life."[2] This quotation holds some truth because we have seen how repeated actions influence behavior. Many times, it is the repeated act that forms a habit, and this habit influences an attitude or opinion. As a result, cultures and ultimately worldviews are influenced.

We also say "You are what you eat." Again, it is not so much the impact of a single meal that we might reference; it is the diet of the individual over a prolonged period. What is it that is being consumed regularly? These food items define the health of the individual. They play a major role in how he lives and even if he lives. For healthier lifestyles we are advised by medical doctors to eat organic produce consistently.

Titus 2 admonishes the saints to be consistent in living because it is a reflection on the faith. If we live by faith, then this belief should be evident in our daily chores. In everything that we do, we should have the doctrine of Christ as our influence. Our steps should be ordered by God's Word. There is no getting around it. We should be careful to consult the scriptures regularly for advice in handling situations or in response to life itself. When we arrive at a godly resolve, we must apply it quickly.

In so doing, we promote our relationship with the Lord Jesus Christ. There is no doubt that we must be careful to do what the Word of God says at all times. Continued commitment to being diligent and obedient will usher the believer to the place where she becomes a friend of God. We show our love and devotion by the frequency with which we enjoy or engage in prayer and fellowship with God. The relationship grows as fellowship increases.

How do we become consistent in our walk with God? The question is, do we really wish to be?

> For where your treasure is, there will your heart be also.
> (Matthew 6:21)

---

[2] Abdol Rauf, "20 Consistency Quotes that Will Bring Consistency I You," *All about Quotes and Life* (blog), October 25, 2013, https://abdolrauf.wordpress.com/2013/10/25/consistency-quotes-about-consistency/.

What we value most, we invest in. We spend time and give of our resources. When we are in love with the Father, we spend time in His presence regularly and give of our talents, time, and oftentimes finances to promote the kingdom of God. So, we are challenged to love God above all influences. We must consider what is most valuable to us, and our thoughts should conform to the concluded decision. Our challenge now is to align every thought so it is held in obedience of Christ. Find pleasure in communicating with God. Further, think about your time in prayer. Consider the words shared in devotion and the key moment of inspiration. This will motivate you to continue in prayer and live a life pleasing to God.

To be consistent, it is understood that we must purpose that every part of our being lines up with our need to be consistent. Our will to connect with God must be strong. Read scriptures. Memorize them and repeat them often to renew your thoughts; this will strengthen the will to want to please God. This process will also help you to speak His Word and also motivate you to live it.

What helps me often is to set aside a specific time to do things. Devotions may be read at a specific time each morning. This time would be respected for devotions every day. Emotions, other commitments, and to some degree illness will never prevent devotions each morning. I do this religiously each morning, understanding that there may situations that will push the prayer time to a bit later or earlier. Sometimes this might happen, so to set hard, fixed rules may not be the best thing at all times. Evaluate this every time. However, generally, desire to pray each day and set a specific time, morning or evening. This helps.

All Issues Come from the Heart

> Keep your heart with all diligence; for out of it are the issues of life.

> —Proverbs 4:23

Holiness is not an option for followers of Christ. It is how we live. There is a distinct difference in life for the believer and life for the unsaved, and that is the purity that Jesus Christ's death afforded to us. Paul admonished believers to sing, to think about the scriptures they read, and most of all to live them. This, he knew, came about by aligning our thoughts with the Word of God. As we think the Word, most likely we will live it. The multiple issues we face in our lives are all directly related to the condition of our hearts. So, we see that the condition of our hearts either illuminates our path or makes it obscure.

Whatever the struggle faced in life, it originated in the heart. We cultivate emotions, opinions, and thoughts in the mind. When the heart suggests a behavior or reaction, it is most likely that the body will respond in agreement. Should, for example, the heart conclude that the death of a loved one is tragic, then one is most likely to see tears and gestures of sorrow. Perception will determine how we respond in any situation.

> For as he thinks in his heart, so is he: Eat and drink, said he to you; but his heart is not with you. (Proverbs 23:7)

How committed or uncommitted we are to holiness is established within our hearts. If envy and strife are lodged in our hearts, the only thing that will come out when challenged is sin. It is important to cleanse ourselves through the Word every day.

> Let all bitterness, and wrath, and anger, and clamor, and evil speaking, be put away from you, with all malice:
>
> And be you kind one to another, tenderhearted, forgiving one another, even as God for Christ's sake has forgiven you. (Ephesians 4:31–32)

Our responsibility is to be like Christ. We should be holy even as He is holy. Sin should not be permitted to remain within our lives.

> Let not sin therefore reign in your mortal body, that you should obey it in the lusts thereof.
>
> Neither yield you your members as instruments of unrighteousness to sin: but yield yourselves to God, as

those that are alive from the dead, and your members as instruments of righteousness to God.

For sin shall not have dominion over you: for you are not under the law, but under grace.

What then? shall we sin, because we are not under the law, but under grace? God forbid.

Know you not, that to whom you yield yourselves servants to obey, his servants you are to whom you obey; whether of sin to death, or of obedience to righteousness?

But God be thanked, that you were the servants of sin, but you have obeyed from the heart that form of doctrine which was delivered you.

Being then made free from sin, you became the servants of righteousness.

I speak after the manner of men because of the infirmity of your flesh: for as you have yielded your members servants to uncleanness and to iniquity to iniquity; even so now yield your members servants to righteousness to holiness.

For when you were the servants of sin, you were free from righteousness.

What fruit had you then in those things whereof you are now ashamed? for the end of those things is death.

But now being made free from sin, and become servants to God, you have your fruit to holiness, and the end everlasting life.

For the wages of sin is death; but the gift of God is eternal life through Jesus Christ our Lord. (Romans 6:12–23)

What Defiles a Person Is What Comes Out of the Mouth

> Not that which goes into the mouth defiles a man; but that which comes out of the mouth, this defiles a man.

—Matthew 15:11

We are expected to be very alert and aware of the challenges we face each day. As we guard our hearts and our thoughts and restrict our engagement in anything that is not of God, we should also purge everything that is not of God. In this manner, when we react to a situation, the Word will have already gone before us, so our response more than likely will be godly.

* * *

Prayer

> Father, I confess that I am a sinner. I have not walked in holiness. I have compromised the faith by my way of life and have disappointed You. Please forgive me. Help me to value You above all things. Reveal Your truth that I might walk circumspectly before You. Allow Your Word to be a two-edged sword in my life, cutting away everything that is not of You. I desire to please You, to draw closer to You. Help me to see Your worth. As You reveal the truth of who You are to me, let my soul cling to You, Father. Make us one. Cleanse me from all filthiness of the flesh. Create in me a clean heart, and renew Your Spirit within me.

In the name of Jesus Christ, I pray.

Amen.

Declaration

I treasure the very essence of who God is. I value His counsel, His truth, and His righteousness, and I declare this day that each day I live I will run deeper into Him. I will follow His guidance and seek Him diligently. I will not waver but, fully persuaded, will live what He says in the scriptures. I will be built continuously on His righteous foundation and rejoice in Him.

Sin will not reign in my body. Daily I will present my body as a living sacrifice, holy and acceptable because it is my reasonable service.

Right now, I lay aside every sin and the weight that so easily besets me.

I will continue to run this race with patience, looking to You, Jesus, the author and finisher of my faith.

CHAPTER 10
Sacrifices Must Be Made

And he said to them all, If any man will come after me, let him deny himself, and take up his cross daily, and follow me.

—Luke 9:23

Jesus admonished His disciples that if they were interested in ministry or rather patterning their lives after His example, they were expected to follow Him with the hardship that comes along with it. The cross is a symbol of difficulties, of hardship, and of struggle. It is a symbol also of breakthrough, of power, and of hope. It clearly symbolizes the power of God to reach a human being wherever he or she may be. What God is telling those who wish to serve Him is that we must leave everything we are familiar with and explore the challenges in a relationship with Him. Jesus made this clear in many of His admonitions. Repeatedly He said that it is not easy to live a life that is set apart.

> And he said to them all, If any man will come after me, let him deny himself, and take up his cross daily, and follow me. (Luke 9:23)

However, it is clear also, and according to Luke, it is a personal choice He freely allows everyone to make. And He makes it clear that there must be a loss. He also indicates that there is no pleasing of the flesh.

We must pay close attention to His directives and the need for the kingdom. To follow Christ means that we will seek to please Him and be like Him, as opposed to considering personal needs. Firstly, sometimes it may be that because of the ministry, the Lord may have us spend time in service to His people rather than joining some social club to further opportunities in business or just to empower us socially. We must make a decision. I clearly understand that we will be expected to maintain this decision by our commitment to the cause of Christ. In our sacrificing and our giving up our offering to the Lord, He is expecting us to give ourselves.

> I beseech you therefore, brothers, by the mercies of God, that you present your bodies a living sacrifice, holy, acceptable to God, which is your reasonable service. (Romans 12:1)

This is an interesting revelation I found when in prayer with the Lord, and I realized that this is exactly what God is expecting according to His Word when He admonishes us to present our bodies as a living sacrifice.

I was inquiring about paying tithes, and I found out something rather interesting and mind-blowing at the same time—but I am convinced that it is the truth, and it is connected with the principle of obedience.

Once we have given our lives to the Lord and accepted His leadership and His guidance, we have completely given ourselves to Him. There is a famous hymn that we often sing:

> I surrender all.

> All to Jesus I surrender,

> All to him I freely give.

It speaks about complete submission in response to Romans 12, which insists we surrender our bodies as a living sacrifice. In sacrificing, we give everything—everything in life, energy, art, talent, academic pursuits, passions, and our desires, that is, everything that concerns us. So, then our lives are not become our own. The scripture says we are bought with a price.

> For you are bought with a price: therefore glorify God in your body, and in your spirit, which are God's. (1 Corinthians 6:20)

Now this means that everything we do really, because of the redemption of Christ, belongs to Christ. It is a privilege that He gives us the free will to choose. How we dedicate our lives, to whom we dedicate our lives, and ultimately to what degree we do this is our choice. It is fair to conclude that living for every believer is because of the blood of Jesus Christ, the blood that He shed for us on Calvary. Everything that we live for as a result, and what area offers benefits or yields results, belongs to God. In the same way, every debt that we accumulate as a result of the decisions we make for the life that we live belongs to God. Why? He has redeemed us and we are His.

> In whom we have redemption through his blood, the forgiveness of sins, according to the riches of his grace. (Ephesians 1:7)

So, as I was saying, greater understanding of the rules, for me, caused truth to resonate in my spirit. This truth tells me, or rather I draw the conclusion, that it is a blessing that the Almighty would allow us in a redeemed state to still have the opportunity to make our own decisions and to choose what we wish when we wish. This is a statement of the mighty great love He has for us. The reality is that we own nothing.

I am reminded of studies I have done on the North American slave trade. When factors captured African nationals, the next step was to transport them to the New World to be sold as slaves. There was no telling what would happen after plantation owners purchased them. For some slaves, they were treated fairly but generally they were overworked. It was not until all slaves were emancipated by law in the United States that they had freedom to do and go as they pleased. This is not so in the kingdom of God. With the act of redemption resulting from the shed blood of Jesus Christ, we are free. This freedom, however, is in the framework of the scriptures. Paul said that even though he had liberty to do all things, he chose not to that he might bring glory to the name of God.

> All things are lawful for me, but all things are not expedient: all things are lawful for me, but all things edify not. (1 Corinthians 10:23)

Finally, I will wrap up by offering a complete understanding of this point on redemption. My position is that we own nothing. Everything that we acquire, materially, academically, and socially, because of the fact that God gave His life to us, all belongs to Him. Nothing we acquire, nothing we own, really belongs to us. He permits these things in our lives. He permits these things to be placed in our care and expects that with His having allowed us the privilege, we will invest time and effort and multiply these resources for His glory. But they are His, not ours, and they should be available every time and anytime for His redistribution or His use.

> And to one he gave five talents, to another two, and to another one; to every man according to his several ability; and straightway took his journey. (Matthew 25:15)

Sow

> In the morning sow your seed, and in the evening withhold not your hand: for you know not whether shall prosper, either this or that, or whether they both shall be alike good.

—Ecclesiastes 11:6

Definition

Sow as a verb (used with object), *sowed*, *sown* or *sowed*, *sowing*, is defined as follows:

- To scatter (seed) over land, earth, etc., for growth; plant.
- To plant seed for: to sow a crop.
- To scatter seed over (land, earth, etc.) for the purpose of growth.
- To implant, introduce, or promulgate; seek to propagate or extend; disseminate: to sow distrust or dissension.
- To strew or sprinkle with anything.

  Sow as a verb (used without object), *sowed*, *sown* or *sowed*, *sowing*, is defined as follows:

- To sow seed, as for the production of a crop.[3]

To sow spiritually, we give of our resources to advance the kingdom of God. This release of resources is done with an expectation from God. The believer gives of himself by faith. This giving is generally, in these modern times, in the form of finances. I have heard of people sowing many other material assets. While giving, a person petitions God for favor in a specific named area. It is a way of breaking barriers that prevents the release of answers to prayer.

---

[3] Dictionary.com, s.v. "sow," https://www.dictionary.com/browse/sow#:~:text=verb%20(used%20with%20object)%2C,.%2C%20for%20growth%3B%20plant.&text=to%20scatter%20seed%20over%20(land,to%20sow%20distrust%20or%20dissension.

The comparison would be a farmer tilling the soil and then planting his crop. The farmer prepares the ground and then puts the seed for the specific crop he is expecting to harvest into the earth. He waters this seed, and from time to time he weeds to ensure that only the desired crop is allowed to grow in the soil.

Faith, prayer, and obedience are the components of care a believer would give to the act of sowing. No matter where she sows or what she sows, she unlocks the door to her breakthrough by believing the Word of God. Care must be taken not to look to the leaders in the church but to look solely and only to God.

Why Sow?

Below are some scriptures that will assist in understanding God's intended purpose.

In the morning sow your seed, and in the evening withhold not your hand: for you know not whether shall prosper, either this or that, or whether they both shall be alike good.

—Ecclesiastes 11:6

For he that sows to his flesh shall of the flesh reap corruption; but he that sows to the Spirit shall of the Spirit reap life everlasting.

—Galatians 6:8

I have showed you all things, how that so laboring you ought to support the weak, and to remember the words of the Lord Jesus, how he said, It is more blessed to give than to receive.

—Acts 20:35

Then Isaac sowed in that land, and received in the same year an hundred times: and the Lord blessed him.

—Genesis 26:12

In the morning sow your seed, and in the evening withhold not your hand: for you know not whether shall prosper, either this or that, or whether they both shall be alike good.

—Ecclesiastes 11:6

Be not deceived; God is not mocked: for whatever a man sows, that shall he also reap.

—Galatians 6:7

But this I say, He which sows sparingly shall reap also sparingly; and he which sows bountifully shall reap also bountifully.

—2 Corinthians 9:6

The Grounds in Which to Sow

The Lord provides a guide to identify the prospects of being rewarded as a result of choosing the environment or opportunity to sow. Let's look at Mark chapter four for insight.

> And it came to pass, as he sowed, some fell by the way side, and the fowls of the air came and devoured it up.
>
> And some fell on stony ground, where it had not much earth; and immediately it sprang up, because it had no depth of earth:

But when the sun was up, it was scorched; and because it had no root, it withered away.

And some fell among thorns, and the thorns grew up, and choked it, and it yielded no fruit.

And other fell on good ground, and did yield fruit that sprang up and increased; and brought forth, some thirty, and some sixty, and some an hundred.

And he said to them, He that has ears to hear, let him hear.

And when he was alone, they that were about him with the twelve asked of him the parable.

And he said to them, To you it is given to know the mystery of the kingdom of God: but to them that are without, all these things are done in parables:

That seeing they may see, and not perceive; and hearing they may hear, and not understand; lest at any time they should be converted, and their sins should be forgiven them.

And he said to them, Know you not this parable? and how then will you know all parables?

The sower sows the word.

And these are they by the way side, where the word is sown; but when they have heard, Satan comes immediately, and takes away the word that was sown in their hearts.

And these are they likewise which are sown on stony ground; who, when they have heard the word, immediately receive it with gladness;

And have no root in themselves, and so endure but for a time: afterward, when affliction or persecution rises for the word's sake, immediately they are offended.

And these are they which are sown among thorns; such as hear the word,

And the cares of this world, and the deceitfulness of riches, and the lusts of other things entering in, choke the word, and it becomes unfruitful.

And these are they which are sown on good ground; such as hear the word, and receive it, and bring forth fruit, some thirty times, some sixty, and some an hundred.

—Mark 4:4–20

What Is Good Ground?

Oftentimes we refer to a congregation or a ministry as good ground. This simply implies that the leadership has a consistent relationship with the Lord Jesus Christ. The leader, given his support in God's work, is endeavoring to live a life above reproof. In addition, it also suggests that the finances of the church are being audited and used to pay for the ministry expenses and the needs of the saints according to the record in Acts of the Apostles.

Good ground does not suggest that the bishop is living the lifestyle of the rich and famous. This is not the teaching of the early church. However, it is about the love of Christ dwelling among God's people. Good ground describes a community of people caring for the things that move God— not materialism, but the redemption of the lost.

Examples from Scripture of People Sowing

Then Isaac sowed in that land, and received in the same year an hundred times: and the Lord blessed him.

And the man waxed great, and went forward, and grew until he became very great.

—Genesis 26:12–13

And God said, Let the earth bring forth grass, the herb yielding seed, and the fruit tree yielding fruit after his kind, whose seed is in itself, on the earth: and it was so.

—Genesis 1:11

Now he that ministers seed to the sower both minister bread for your food, and multiply your seed sown, and increase the fruits of your righteousness.

—2 Corinthians 9:10

Then Isaac sowed in that land, and received in the same year an hundred times: and the Lord blessed him.

—Genesis 26:12

Tithe

Bring you all the tithes into the storehouse, that there may be meat in my house, and prove me now herewith, said the Lord of hosts, if I will not open you the windows of heaven, and pour you out a blessing, that there shall not be room enough to receive it.

—Malachi 3:10

The tithe is 10 percent of one's annual income. Depending on the environment, the individual's choice, or the person's work compensation policies, this presentation of tithes may not occur annually. It may occur weekly or biweekly, monthly, or even quarterly. The important thing is that the tenth is returned to further the gospel. This tenth of annual earnings is presented to the local church to assist with the financial costs of the assembly ministering to the body of Christ.

Beginning with the building, it may aid in payment of a rental or lease agreement or perhaps a mortgage. Other overhead expenditures such as utilities are electricity, water, gas, telephone, internet, and alarm security. Factors such as media production may be considered, depending on the need of the church. There is also the concern for maintenance of the worship environment. This may include cleaning and maintenance of any part of the structure (or the whole thing). The assembly may have staff, training sessions, guest presenters, or musicians who all require payment for services rendered.

It is often said among devoted Christians that the tenth is a portion of God blessings. Further, all of who we are and what we earn belongs to God. So should the question really be asked, "How much belongs to God?" The true answer is, "Everything." The scripture declares the He gave us the power to get wealth.

I have continuously stressed *presented* instead of *given* when referring to the tenth, or tithe, because I believe that everything belongs to God. The entire 100 percent is His. I do not believe we have the capacity to own anything. It is His world, His creation, His earth, and therefore His resources, His wood coming from His trees, etc. You get the idea. He is gracious to permit us to use these things so that we will have a comfortable life. He charged humankind to dominate in Genesis 1. It is upon this fact that I affirm that everything belongs to God. The scripture reminds us that we are not our own; we are bought with a price. Jesus shared His blood to redeem us to Himself. We are His. Our life, our wealth, is His. It's a wonder we only discuss "paying" the tithe, when God truly owns the entire portion. He permits us as managers to do as we wish with the 90 percent that is His also. So, it's not a matter of paying, because it already belongs to Him.

The parable of the five talents infers to us that we should use the resources to increase wealth while we have the opportunity. He, as we see from His instructions to Adam and Eve, left humankind as caretakers of the earth. We do not own the earth, but we do have authority to operate as the rightful owners. When we commit our lives fully to Christ, we give Him everything we are. We give Him our present, past, and future. He, at salvation, demands the entire 100 percent! In response to our surrender, He gives us authority to dominate the earth in every area of life. Many of us do it without knowing what this arrangement is all about. We just know the earth is ours to conquer.

What faith! Isn't it wonderful faith the human race possesses—and rightfully so—in God? We buy and sell. We establish cultures and regions. We establish bodies of law to address behaviors and relations in business and family life globally as though we own the things we exclusively manage. We have every confidence that they are our possessions because the paperwork legally affirms this, but we are still only managers with divine authority to dominate and populate. Our faith in this authority makes us to understand that God will not terminate this structure. So, we divide and we conquer, some more than others. Surprisingly, this has become a world effort, regardless of religious persuasion. We believe the earth is ours to dominate. We, Christian, Jew, Muslim, Hindu, Buddhist, and Primal-Indigenous, believe the Lord Jesus. Our actions of buying and selling, living in society, are a response to our faith in Him. It is amazing how we do things and may never consider the true implications. So again, the scripture is true: "To everyone is given a measure of faith." I would further hypothesize based on the foregoing simple truth and ask this question: Is there really such a thing as an atheist?

Make a Covenant with God

The Lord is a covenant God. He seeks to establish relationships with His people to encourage commitment and loyalty (2 Samuel 23:5; Psalm 89:3). He delights in a sustained long-term relationship with believers. It is documented that because of these relationships, children and generations were blessed and were able to pray, reminding God of His relationship with

RELEASING THE OVERCOMER'S ANOINTING

individuals so that they received pardon and were able to benefit from the covenant made.

A covenant is an agreement. Its Latin meaning implies a coming together. The word *testament* has also been used for *covenant*. It is expected that parties make an agreement that is confirmed by a verbal response, an oath. The covenant between God and humankind suggests that both God and humanity agree to certain conditions and procedures. It affects all aspects of humankind's existence. Ultimately, we know the relationship between God and humankind is based on an agreement that God is supreme and has humankind's best interests as His priority. With this in mind, we know that God loves us. He wants us to dominate.

Reminders When Establishing a Covenant

- God will only agree to an agreement based on His Word.
- Do not make an agreement that you do not intend to keep.
- Covenants with God are not easily broken (Hosea 6:7).
- Be honest.
- Making a covenant can and will affect your loved ones.

As a result of your covenant, God will hear and will move on your behalf. The important point is not to forget your vows and to put them before you at all times in prayer and in action. God, as a result of prayer, will tell you exactly what step to take, one after the next. God does not respond to false petitions but to sincerity.

Read through the following passage as an example of how to word a covenant with God:

Jacob Makes a Covenant with God

And Jacob went out from Beersheba, and went toward Haran.

And he lighted on a certain place, and tarried there all night, because the sun was set; and he took of the stones of that place, and put them for his pillows, and lay down in that place to sleep.

And he dreamed, and behold a ladder set up on the earth, and the top of it reached to heaven: and behold the angels of God ascending and descending on it.

And, behold, the Lord stood above it, and said, I am the Lord God of Abraham your father, and the God of Isaac: the land where on you lie, to you will I give it, and to your seed;

And your seed shall be as the dust of the earth, and you shall spread abroad to the west, and to the east, and to the north, and to the south: and in you and in your seed shall all the families of the earth be blessed.

And, behold, I am with you, and will keep you in all places where you go, and will bring you again into this land; for I will not leave you, until I have done that which I have spoken to you of.

And Jacob awaked out of his sleep, and he said, Surely the Lord is in this place; and I knew it not.

And he was afraid, and said, How dreadful is this place! this is none other but the house of God, and this is the gate of heaven.

And Jacob rose up early in the morning, and took the stone that he had put for his pillows, and set it up for a pillar, and poured oil on the top of it.

And he called the name of that place Bethel: but the name of that city was called Luz at the first.

And Jacob vowed a vow, saying, If God will be with me, and will keep me in this way that I go, and will give me bread to eat, and raiment to put on,

So that I come again to my father's house in peace; then shall the Lord be my God:

And this stone, which I have set for a pillar, shall be God's house: and of all that you shall give me I will surely give the tenth to you.

—Genesis 28:10–22

* * *

Prayer

Father, In the name of Jesus, I recognize that in order to walk closely with You, I must value You above those things that I consider important. I admit that I have had many desires and motives that were not in keeping with the principles of Your Word. Today, right now, I denounce them in the name of Jesus.

I align my mind, my will, my spirit, and my passion with Your Word. Create in me a clean heart and renew a right spirit within me. Let me know Your ways, and I shall continually walk in them.

Amen.

Declaration

I declare this day that I am not my own. I have been bought with a price, the precious blood of Jesus Christ. I belong to God. I vow that I will not neglect to give to the work of the Lord financially and by way of any other means afforded to me. Every covenant established between us, I will honor with all sincerity. I will see the fulfillment of the promise and will rejoice as well.

CHAPTER 11
Obey the Specific Instructions of God

If you shall listen to the voice of the Lord your God, to keep his commandments and his statutes which are written in this book of the law, and if you turn to the Lord your God with all your heart, and with all your soul.

—Deuteronomy 30:10

God has a specific order for things. He sits as the overseer and controller of life. As a matter of fact, He is life Himself. He knows what happens next. The sequence of events in our lives is a result of His plan and purpose for our lives. We affect these ordered events when we begin making decisions that are not in keeping with His will for our lives. These decisions are the ones that present challenges, when enacted, and deviate us from our godly assignments. Depending on the nature of our actions, we might find ourselves with greater or fewer obstacles to conquer in order to realign ourselves with divine order.

The Lord may be considered as a divine Father. Numerous scriptures have called Him our Father. In this light, we see that He is concerned about us because we are His children. It is the duty of parents to train their children. This training is extended to all areas of life. They are expected to teach scriptures and explain them. They are expected to teach children how to apply these to daily living. Parents should instruct their children in how to respond to culture based on the Word of God. These instructions enable a child to walk in wisdom. Should these parental instructions be obeyed, a child will lead a productive and successful life.

The instruction given by parents is not only one of guidance and direction. It is also instruction to enforce the instructions or to ensure they are carried out. So, as in many organizations, the family will have measures in place for breach of conduct. There is a level of discipline for disobedience (Romans 11:20, 22). This discipline reminds the child of his or her responsibility to follow parental instructions and directs the child to return to obedience. The scripture has many examples of disobedience being punished by God, the Father of all (Romans 1:28–30).

With correction and instruction, there is also motivation to adhere to Christian principles. Parents have a responsibility to inspire children to serve the Lord and do what is right. They are expected to reward their children for following their instructions. There are numerous promises of blessings arising from obedience in the scriptures. These blessings extend from God's protection to material increase. So parenting is not a hands-off relationship. It is an involved and sacrificial relationship that demands time and communication.

Finally, a parent knows that all instructions may not be carried out by his or her children. In the event that disobedience does happen, parents not only correct but also forgive and are compassionate (Psalm 103:13). This display of forgiveness builds bonds of trust in family members. As for Christians, our faith is reinforced and we become even more convinced in the Lord as sovereign when we see His rewards (Exodus 20:12; Deuteronomy 5:16; Matthew 15:4; Mark 10:19; Ephesians 6:1–3; Colossians 3:20).

> My son, hear the instruction of your father, and forsake
> not the law of your mother. (Proverbs 1:8)

There is something about the honest advice given by people who are more mature and experienced. In most instances, such people help shed light on the gravest of situations. These words of wisdom make it easier to cope, adjust, and overcome. Wisdom shared by people who have already lived our present occurrences somehow saves time and resources. People who care for us, in most instances, will give their best advice to bring us out of our dilemmas. Seniority of our familiar acquaintances, not just acquaintances, has its values.

The referenced scripture admonishes a son to listen to and obey his parents. The bottom line here is that the parents have authority over the child. They are expected to manage their household well and ensure that there is a level of respect and integrity in their home (1 Timothy 3:4).

However, parental advice is more profound. The instructions given by parents are regarded in the scripture as if God Himself were to give instruction. Throughout the Bible, sons and daughters regarded and highly respected their parents' instruction. It was expected that the children would wholeheartedly obey these instructions. There seems to be a divine blessing for obedience to parents and without compromise.

Children Who Obeyed Their Parents in Scripture, and the Reward that Followed

Isaac
Isaac was Abraham's only son in marriage. At the time he was born, both his parents were very old. To secure a wife for Isaac, Abraham sent his

servant to his family. As a result, the oath that they made was fulfilled and Isaac was married to his mother's niece. This made Abraham very happy.

And Abraham was old, and well stricken in age: and the Lord had blessed Abraham in all things.

And Abraham said to his oldest servant of his house, that ruled over all that he had, Put, I pray you, your hand under my thigh:

And I will make you swear by the Lord, the God of heaven, and the God of the earth, that you shall not take a wife to my son of the daughters of the Canaanites, among whom I dwell:

But you shall go to my country, and to my kindred, and take a wife to my son Isaac.

And the servant said to him, Peradventure the woman will not be willing to follow me to this land: must I needs bring your son again to the land from where you came?

And Abraham said to him, Beware you that you bring not my son thither again.

The Lord God of heaven, which took me from my father's house, and from the land of my kindred, and which spoke to me, and that swore to me, saying, To your seed will I give this land; he shall send his angel before you, and you shall take a wife to my son from there.

And if the woman will not be willing to follow you, then you shall be clear from this my oath: only bring not my son thither again.

And the servant put his hand under the thigh of Abraham his master, and swore to him concerning that matter.

And the servant took ten camels of the camels of his master, and departed; for all the goods of his master were in his hand: and he arose, and went to Mesopotamia, to the city of Nahor.

And he made his camels to kneel down without the city by a well of water at the time of the evening, even the time that women go out to draw water.

And he said O Lord God of my master Abraham, I pray you, send me good speed this day, and show kindness to my master Abraham.

Behold, I stand here by the well of water; and the daughters of the men of the city come out to draw water:

And let it come to pass, that the damsel to whom I shall say, Let down your pitcher, I pray you, that I may drink; and she shall say, Drink, and I will give your camels drink also: let the same be she that you have appointed for your servant Isaac; and thereby shall I know that you have showed kindness to my master.

And it came to pass, before he had done speaking, that, behold, Rebekah came out, who was born to Bethuel, son of Milcah, the wife of Nahor, Abraham's brother, with her pitcher on her shoulder.

And the damsel was very fair to look on, a virgin, neither had any man known her: and she went down to the well, and filled her pitcher, and came up.

And the servant ran to meet her, and said, Let me, I pray you, drink a little water of your pitcher.

And she said, Drink, my lord: and she hurried, and let down her pitcher on her hand, and gave him drink.

And when she had done giving him drink, she said, I will draw water for your camels also, until they have done drinking.

And she hurried, and emptied her pitcher into the trough, and ran again to the well to draw water, and drew for all his camels.

And the man wondering at her held his peace, to wit whether the Lord had made his journey prosperous or not.

And it came to pass, as the camels had done drinking, that the man took a golden earring of half a shekel weight, and two bracelets for her hands of ten shekels weight of gold;

And said, Whose daughter are you? tell me, I pray you: is there room in your father's house for us to lodge in?

And she said to him, I am the daughter of Bethuel the son of Milcah, which she bore to Nahor.

She said moreover to him, We have both straw and provender enough, and room to lodge in.

And the man bowed down his head, and worshipped the Lord.

And he said, Blessed be the Lord God of my master Abraham, who has not left destitute my master of his mercy and his truth: I being in the way, the Lord led me to the house of my master's brothers.

And the damsel ran, and told them of her mother's house these things.

And Rebekah had a brother, and his name was Laban: and Laban ran out to the man, to the well.

And it came to pass, when he saw the earring and bracelets on his sister's hands, and when he heard the words of Rebekah his sister, saying, Thus spoke the man to me; that he came to the man; and, behold, he stood by the camels at the well.

And he said, Come in, you blessed of the Lord; why stand you without? for I have prepared the house, and room for the camels.

And the man came into the house: and he ungirded his camels, and gave straw and provender for the camels, and water to wash his feet, and the men's feet that were with him.

And there was set meat before him to eat: but he said, I will not eat, until I have told my errand. And he said, Speak on.

And he said, I am Abraham's servant.

And the Lord has blessed my master greatly; and he is become great: and he has given him flocks, and herds, and silver, and gold, and menservants, and maidservants, and camels, and asses.

And Sarah my master's wife bore a son to my master when she was old: and to him has he given all that he has.

And my master made me swear, saying, You shall not take a wife to my son of the daughters of the Canaanites, in whose land I dwell:

But you shall go to my father's house, and to my kindred, and take a wife to my son.

And I said to my master, Peradventure the woman will not follow me.

And he said to me, The Lord, before whom I walk, will send his angel with you, and prosper your way; and you shall take a wife for my son of my kindred, and of my father's house:

Then shall you be clear from this my oath, when you come to my kindred; and if they give not you one, you shall be clear from my oath.

And I came this day to the well, and said, O Lord God of my master Abraham, if now you do prosper my way which I go:

Behold, I stand by the well of water; and it shall come to pass, that when the virgin comes forth to draw water, and I say to her, Give me, I pray you, a little water of your pitcher to drink;

And she say to me, Both drink you, and I will also draw for your camels: let the same be the woman whom the Lord has appointed out for my master's son.

And before I had done speaking in my heart, behold, Rebekah came forth with her pitcher on her shoulder; and she went down to the well, and drew water: and I said to her, Let me drink, I pray you.

And she made haste, and let down her pitcher from her shoulder, and said, Drink, and I will give your camels drink also: so I drank, and she made the camels drink also.

And I asked her, and said, Whose daughter are you? And she said, the daughter of Bethuel, Nahor's son, whom

Milcah bore to him: and I put the earring on her face, and the bracelets on her hands.

And I bowed down my head, and worshipped the Lord, and blessed the Lord God of my master Abraham, which had led me in the right way to take my master's brother's daughter to his son.

And now if you will deal kindly and truly with my master, tell me: and if not, tell me; that I may turn to the right hand, or to the left.

Then Laban and Bethuel answered and said, The thing proceeds from the Lord: we cannot speak to you bad or good.

Behold, Rebekah is before you, take her, and go, and let her be your master's son's wife, as the Lord has spoken.

And it came to pass, that, when Abraham's servant heard their words, he worshipped the Lord, bowing himself to the earth.

And the servant brought forth jewels of silver, and jewels of gold, and raiment, and gave them to Rebekah: he gave also to her brother and to her mother precious things.

And they did eat and drink, he and the men that were with him, and tarried all night; and they rose up in the morning, and he said, Send me away to my master.

And her brother and her mother said, Let the damsel abide with us a few days, at the least ten; after that she shall go.

And he said to them, Hinder me not, seeing the Lord has prospered my way; send me away that I may go to my master.

And they said, We will call the damsel, and inquire at her mouth.

And they called Rebekah, and said to her, Will you go with this man? And she said, I will go.

And they sent away Rebekah their sister, and her nurse, and Abraham's servant, and his men.

And they blessed Rebekah, and said to her, You are our sister, be you the mother of thousands of millions, and let your seed possess the gate of those which hate them.

And Rebekah arose, and her damsels, and they rode on the camels, and followed the man: and the servant took Rebekah, and went his way.

And Isaac came from the way of the well Lahairoi; for he dwelled in the south country.

And Isaac went out to meditate in the field at the eventide: and he lifted up his eyes, and saw, and, behold, the camels were coming.

And Rebekah lifted up her eyes, and when she saw Isaac, she lighted off the camel.

For she had said to the servant, What man is this that walks in the field to meet us? And the servant had said, It is my master: therefore she took a veil, and covered herself.

And the servant told Isaac all things that he had done.

And Isaac brought her into his mother Sarah's tent, and took Rebekah, and she became his wife; and he loved her: and Isaac was comforted after his mother's death. (Genesis 24:1–67)

Jacob

Jacob was one of the twins born to Rachel after a long period of her waiting to have a child for her husband. Jacob's brother Esau was the firstborn but lost his birthright to Jacob in their exchange for porridge. Jacob managed to take not only Esau's birthright but also his blessing. This made Esau very bitter; he vowed to kill Jacob immediately after his father's death. Rebecca heard this and gave Jacob instructions to go to her brother and find a wife there. He did find a wife. As a matter of fact, he married two of Laban's daughters. God was with Jacob and blessed him. Everything his hands touched was blessed. Eventually he and his brother were reunited in peace.

> And Rebekah spoke to Jacob her son, saying, Behold, I heard your father speak to Esau your brother, saying,
>
> Bring me venison, and make me savoury meat, that I may eat, and bless you before the Lord before my death.
>
> Now therefore, my son, obey my voice according to that which I command you.
>
> Go now to the flock, and fetch me from there two good kids of the goats; and I will make them savoury meat for your father, such as he loves:
>
> And you shall bring it to your father, that he may eat, and that he may bless you before his death.
>
> And Jacob said to Rebekah his mother, Behold, Esau my brother is a hairy man, and I am a smooth man:
>
> My father peradventure will feel me, and I shall seem to him as a deceiver; and I shall bring a curse on me, and not a blessing.
>
> And his mother said to him, On me be your curse, my son: only obey my voice, and go fetch me them.

And he went, and fetched, and brought them to his mother: and his mother made savoury meat, such as his father loved.

And Rebekah took goodly raiment of her oldest son Esau, which were with her in the house, and put them on Jacob her younger son:

And she put the skins of the kids of the goats on his hands, and on the smooth of his neck:

And she gave the savoury meat and the bread, which she had prepared, into the hand of her son Jacob.

And he came to his father, and said, My father: and he said, Here am I; who are you, my son?

And Jacob said to his father, I am Esau your first born; I have done according as you bade me: arise, I pray you, sit and eat of my venison, that your soul may bless me.

And Isaac said to his son, How is it that you have found it so quickly, my son? And he said, Because the Lord your God brought it to me.

And Isaac said to Jacob, Come near, I pray you, that I may feel you, my son, whether you be my very son Esau or not.

And Jacob went near to Isaac his father; and he felt him, and said, The voice is Jacob's voice, but the hands are the hands of Esau.

And he discerned him not, because his hands were hairy, as his brother Esau's hands: so he blessed him.

And he said, Are you my very son Esau? And he said, I am.

And he said, Bring it near to me, and I will eat of my son's venison, that my soul may bless you. And he brought it near to him, and he did eat: and he brought him wine and he drank.

And his father Isaac said to him, Come near now, and kiss me, my son.

And he came near, and kissed him: and he smelled the smell of his raiment, and blessed him, and said, See, the smell of my son is as the smell of a field which the Lord has blessed:

Therefore God give you of the dew of heaven, and the fatness of the earth, and plenty of corn and wine:

Let people serve you, and nations bow down to you: be lord over your brothers, and let your mother's sons bow down to you: cursed be every one that curses you, and blessed be he that blesses you.

And it came to pass, as soon as Isaac had made an end of blessing Jacob, and Jacob was yet scarce gone out from the presence of Isaac his father, that Esau his brother came in from his hunting.

And he also had made savoury meat, and brought it to his father, and said to his father, Let my father arise, and eat of his son's venison, that your soul may bless me.

And Isaac his father said to him, Who are you? And he said, I am your son, your firstborn Esau.

And Isaac trembled very exceedingly, and said, Who? where is he that has taken venison, and brought it me, and I have eaten of all before you came, and have blessed him? yes, and he shall be blessed.

And when Esau heard the words of his father, he cried with a great and exceeding bitter cry, and said to his father, Bless me, even me also, O my father.

And he said, Your brother came with subtlety, and has taken away your blessing.

And he said, Is not he rightly named Jacob? for he has supplanted me these two times: he took away my birthright; and, behold, now he has taken away my blessing. And he said, Have you not reserved a blessing for me?

And Isaac answered and said to Esau, Behold, I have made him your lord, and all his brothers have I given to him for servants; and with corn and wine have I sustained him: and what shall I do now to you, my son?

And Esau said to his father, Have you but one blessing, my father? bless me, even me also, O my father. And Esau lifted up his voice, and wept.

And Isaac his father answered and said to him, Behold, your dwelling shall be the fatness of the earth, and of the dew of heaven from above;

And by your sword shall you live, and shall serve your brother; and it shall come to pass when you shall have the dominion, that you shall break his yoke from off your neck.

And Esau hated Jacob because of the blessing with which his father blessed him: and Esau said in his heart, The days of mourning for my father are at hand; then will I slay my brother Jacob.

And these words of Esau her elder son were told to Rebekah: and she sent and called Jacob her younger son, and said to him, Behold, your brother Esau, as touching you, does comfort himself, purposing to kill you.

Now therefore, my son, obey my voice; arise, flee you to Laban my brother to Haran;

And tarry with him a few days, until your brother's fury turn away;

Until your brother's anger turn away from you, and he forget that which you have done to him: then I will send, and fetch you from there: why should I be deprived also of you both in one day?

And Rebekah said to Isaac, I am weary of my life because of the daughters of Heth: if Jacob take a wife of the daughters of Heth, such as these which are of the daughters of the land, what good shall my life do me? (Genesis 27:6–46)

The Lord insists that He personally will guide the servant. In His instructions, according to the text, there will be clear directives as to the directions and path the believer should follow. I believe these are specific to the believer's circumstance and personality. The Lord takes into account the entire person. His instruction is not only in the knowledge of scripture but also in its application in our daily lives. He has a personal interest in our well-being. His nature as protector, guide, guard, and provider is evident in these few words. God is often revered as an all-seeing Deity who looks over the affairs of His people. He sees all and knows all. So therefore, from an informed position, He gives the believer instructions for empowerment. This ensures success.

The Lord desires that we would prosper and be in good health. He therefore takes a personal approach to ensuring our success in all areas of our lives.

You see then how that by works a man is justified, and not by faith only. (James 2:24)

If we believe, then we act upon our beliefs. Believing is one thing, but our actions confirm our beliefs. There is something about showing by demonstration that affirms our faith in Christ. It also bonds individuals by way of a common interest.

> Was not Abraham our father justified by works, when he had offered Isaac his son on the altar?
>
> See you how faith worked with his works, and by works was faith made perfect?
>
> And the scripture was fulfilled which said, Abraham believed God, and it was imputed to him for righteousness: and he was called the Friend of God.
>
> You see then how that by works a man is justified, and not by faith only.
>
> Likewise also was not Rahab the harlot justified by works, when she had received the messengers, and had sent them out another way?
>
> For as the body without the spirit is dead, so faith without works is dead also. (James 2:21–26)

Abraham trusted God's instructions. When he was asked to sacrifice his only child in wedlock, he did not hesitate to do so. God, seeing his heart toward Him, did not permit Abraham to complete the sacrifice of his son. God instead provided a ram for Abraham. This was a very courageous and obedient act for Abraham. He had waited so many years and had tried to provide an heir through a servant. Yet he believed God's promise.

Rahab, again, understood that she was doing good as she permitted the spies Joshua had sent out to view the land to pass through her house and then over the wall. When we believe, we activate this system of beliefs by doing something. This something involves action. Action, when accumulated, is a testament to what is believed.

He that has my commandments, and keeps them, he it is
that loves me: and he that loves me shall be loved of my
Father, and I will love him, and will manifest myself to
him. (John 14:21)

Our love for the Lord is determined by our commitment to His divine
order. Our obedience to the keeping of the Word of God will always be an
indication of our love for God. One can further deduce that obedience is
the proof of intimacy with God. We learn what He desires through careful
and continued study of His Word, and we apply this wholeheartedly. Study
and meditation enable us to understand who He is and, as a result, who
we are. Consequently, knowing what He wants and who He is, we are
expected to please Him.

As a result of our obedience, we will be in favor with not only
Jesus Christ but also the Father. The Trinity has united characteristics.
Obedience affirms the relationship between the believer and the Lord. It
also reveals His love.

Obedience and devotion to God's covenant provides an atmosphere
of trust. God sees that He can trust His children when they are obedient
to Him. As a result, He will reveal His secrets to them. The revealing of
divine secrets is not just a believer's increasing in knowledge and wisdom. It
is more than this. It is the release of the knowledge that gives authority and
power to mortal humankind. It further unites the believer with the Lord
and releases access to the spirit beyond the ordinary. Believers gradually
learn to communicate with God in a more intimate and confident
manner. They have insight into the supernatural and learn how to respond
appropriately as the Lord communicates with them. As the Lord reveals
Himself, the believer understands more and is drawn closer to the Lord.
As he or she grows in understanding the laws of the spirit and becomes
confident in this knowledge, application, and understanding, the believer
begins to see the result of the execution of such power.

Believing the Word, living it, and acting on it brings results. These
results may be current natural events that line up smoothly every day. And
as a result, there is a peace. It may be that there is also wisdom in judgment
to overcome obstacles resulting from life's challenges.

In divinely appointed situations, the miraculous may even occur. The supernatural manifestation of the divine nature of God is often revealed among those who have a lasting relationship with God. At His pleasure, the keys to the release of His presence are activated to bring about change. We experience healing, victory, deliverance, and favor that is anything but ordinary.

> Know you not, that to whom you yield yourselves servants to
> obey, his servants you are to whom you obey; whether of sin
> to death, or of obedience to righteousness? (Romans 6:16)

Servants are expected to revere the policies of their masters. Whoever the master is, whether by our will or as a result of enslavement, we are expected to obey his or her instructions. In the previous verses, the believer is admonished not to allow sin to become a regular occurrence. Sin, as the writer admonished, accumulates, but to the disadvantage of children of God. With willful sin, there is bondage. Sin has an automatic punishment regardless of the promise of grace. This punishment is death. Grace is for the believer, to release him or her from the punishment of death. This is the blessing of the shed blood of Jesus Christ.

The author of Romans, Paul, has a concern he voices with very strong conviction. He corrects believers from creating a pattern of continued willful sin in daily living. Not only does this increase the grace extended, but also it threatens the believer with the possibility of being imprisoned spiritually.

Paul highlights not only the negative outcome of wrong choices but also the God-ordained outcome for obedience to God's Word. This obedience, Paul says, produces righteousness in the believer. Righteousness comes from God. It cannot be attained by our works. Obedience for the believer shows the Lord our intent. It reveals the true condition of our hearts. As this scripture suggests, it affirms our loyalty either to good or evil. As the choice is free, our allegiance is also a personal decision. The consequences of our decision, however, will be ours to bear also.

The choice is explained carefully to us as Paul makes a case as to why we should be loyal to one faith only. Without making a choice, the author explains, our actions determine what we would have chosen. You see, the agreement between good and evil had been established far before our time. We cannot change this truth, but we can decide what we wish for the direction of our lives.

Death is a curse. It may not necessarily be a physical death. Death may affect the physical for the duration of the sin and may last beyond given the punishment affixed to the sin. And reoccurrences can only increase the problem. They may even create other problems.

God's Instruction to Noah

> And the Lord said to Noah, Come you and all your house into the ark; for you have I seen righteous before me in this generation.
>
> Of every clean beast you shall take to you by sevens, the male and his female: and of beasts that are not clean by two, the male and his female.
>
> Of fowls also of the air by sevens, the male and the female; to keep seed alive on the face of all the earth.
>
> For yet seven days, and I will cause it to rain on the earth forty days and forty nights; and every living substance that I have made will I destroy from off the face of the earth.
>
> And Noah did according to all that the Lord commanded him.
>
> And Noah was six hundred years old when the flood of waters was on the earth.
>
> —Genesis 7:1–6

God gave Noah instructions to build an ark. He was to build a boat and collect two animals of the same species, a male and a female. He was rejected by his neighbors, but the animals and his family all went into the ark as God had commanded. As a result, the Flood did come and the earth was completely cleansed. All living in the ark survived, and those who had remained without died.

The Flood eventually subsided, and the earth eventually began to be renewed. Noah's family survived and were blessed accordingly.

Naaman Washes in the River Jordan

And Elisha sent a messenger to him, saying, Go and wash in Jordan seven times, and your flesh shall come again to you, and you shall be clean.

—2 Kings 5:10

These instructions may have been considered to be condescending. However, the prophet gave instructions to the sick to wash in the Jordan River seven times. The question is "Why did he not send the individual to bathe in a cleaner river when there were other options?" The Jordan was a muddy river. But the individual listened and received the healing that was sought.

Jesus Asked for Bread and Fish

And they say to him, We have here but five loaves, and two fishes.

He said, Bring them here to me.

And he commanded the multitude to sit down on the grass, and took the five loaves, and the two fishes, and looking up to heaven, he blessed, and broke, and gave the loaves to his disciples, and the disciples to the multitude.

And they did all eat, and were filled: and they took up of the fragments that remained twelve baskets full.

—Matthew 14:17–20

God's way of provision is not ours. We respond to what we see. God is the Creator of all and knows all. He understands everything about our DNA and can command increase, death, or life with His spoken Word. So, asking for the fish and bread was just the beginning of fulfilling the need of the assembled group. Jesus knew that His spoken word would multiply the five loaves and two fish. Obedience here resulted in an overwhelming amount of food.

Joshua Marching around the Walls of Jericho

And the Lord said unto Joshua, See, I have given into thine hand Jericho, and the king thereof, and the mighty men of valour.

And ye shall compass the city, all ye men of war, and go round about the city once. Thus shalt thou do six days.

And seven priests shall bear before the ark seven trumpets of rams' horns: and the seventh day ye shall compass the city seven times, and the priests shall blow with the trumpets.

And it shall come to pass, that when they make a long blast with the ram's horn, and when ye hear the sound of the trumpet, all the people shall shout with a great shout; and the wall of the city shall fall down flat, and the people shall ascend up every man straight before him.

—Joshua 6:2–5

The feat experienced by the Israelites would not have been possible without obedience. It was nothing but miraculous. Joshua gave God's instructions to the host who accompanied him. They obeyed, and the Lord honored His promise to them. The fortified walls of Jericho came down.

Water to Wine

> And both Jesus was called, and his disciples, to the marriage.
>
> And when they wanted wine, the mother of Jesus said to him, They have no wine.
>
> Jesus said to her, Woman, what have I to do with you? my hour is not yet come.
>
> His mother said to the servants, Whatever he said to you, do it.
>
> And there were set there six water pots of stone, after the manner of the purifying of the Jews, containing two or three firkins apiece.
>
> Jesus said to them, Fill the water pots with water. And they filled them up to the brim.
>
> And he said to them, Draw out now, and bear to the governor of the feast. And they bore it.
>
> When the ruler of the feast had tasted the water that was made wine, and knew not from where it was: (but the servants which drew the water knew;) the governor of the feast called the bridegroom.
>
> —John 2:5–9

There is often no logic or academic reasoning that will explain creating a completely different beverage made from water alone. There was no process described in the making of the wine. The only process was to have containers filled with water. No other ingredient was added. So, how would it be possible for this water to be turned out after only being poured in and be the best of wine? Obedience is the prerequisite for miracles.

Saul Went to Damascus

> And he said, Who are you, Lord? And the Lord said, I am Jesus whom you persecute: it is hard for you to kick against the pricks.
>
> And he trembling and astonished said, Lord, what will you have me to do? And the Lord said to him, Arise, and go into the city, and it shall be told you what you must do.
>
> —Acts 9:5–6

Saul was responsible for numerous persecutions against the Christian church. His trip to Damascus was an effort to persecute the church, but he had an encounter with the Lord on his journey. This encounter not only blinded him temporarily but also changed his life. The Lord gave him a true picture of their relationship. This picture revealed to Saul the power and authority that he held. In fear, this soldier, known for his cruelty, submitted to God.

Saul's obedience gave birth to a revolution in the faith. This was the open door to the salvation of the Gentiles. People who had no place in the kingdom were given the opportunity with Saul's conversion to now acknowledge the Lord Jesus Christ and be saved.

Take the time to read the following scriptures. They should shed further light on obedience.

> Nevertheless for David's sake did the Lord his God give him a lamp in Jerusalem, to set up his son after him, and to establish Jerusalem. (1 Kings 15:4)

The children of your servants shall continue, and their seed shall be established before you. (Psalm 102:28)

The just man walks in his integrity: his children are blessed after him. (Proverbs 20:7)

And because he loved your fathers, therefore he chose their seed after them, and brought you out in his sight with his mighty power out of Egypt. (Deuteronomy 4:37)

*　　*　　*

Prayer

Father, I have full confidence that You are able to deliver me from every adverse situation. However, not my will but Your will be done in my life. I submit in obedience to Your Word. As You would instruct, I will obey. Provide wisdom, knowledge, and clear instructions that I would apply to my life, Father. It is my desire to see Your fullness. I open my heart, my mind, my eyes, and my ears to Your truth alone. I wait, Jesus, thanking You for Your love.

Amen.

Declaration

I [your name] acknowledge that I am Christ's. I will only listen to the instruction of the true Shepherd. I acknowledge that obedience welcomes Your presence in my life according to John 14:23. I will remain in fellowship with You. I will delight in Your instructions and see Your Word be established.

CHAPTER 12
Burden of Proof

Bring ye all the tithes into the storehouse, that there may be meat in mine house, and prove me now herewith, saith the Lord of hosts, if I will not open you the windows of heaven, and pour you out a blessing, that there shall not be room enough to receive it.

—Malachi 3:10

Prove God—the Burden of Proof Is on Us

> Now therefore fear the Lord, and serve him in sincerity and in truth: and put away the gods which your fathers served on the other side of the flood, and in Egypt; and serve you the Lord.
>
> And if it seem evil to you to serve the Lord, choose you this day whom you will serve; whether the gods which your fathers served that were on the other side of the flood, or the gods of the Amorites, in whose land you dwell: but as for me and my house, we will serve the Lord.
>
> —Joshua 24:14–15

The Lord has instructed me to build our faith through His instruction. In so doing, we will be in a position not only to hear and receive from God for ourselves but also be able to help others and advance the kingdom. I admonish each person under the sound of my voice to listen intently, write notes because these are divine instructions and not the brain child of Darnell L. McIntosh Whymns. But this text is a release of the answer that you have been praying for, for so long, and God has instructed me to show you the path. As you follow His instruction, you will receive a breakthrough.

But the People Who Do Know Their God Shall Be Strong and Do Exploits

The overriding theme that I feel in my spirit for some years is taken from the following:

> And such as do wickedly against the covenant shall he corrupt by flatteries; but the people who do know their God shall be strong, and do exploits. (Daniel 11:32)

So, I challenge you to study this verse, memorize it, and endeavor to know Him. With this in mind, it is my assignment to walk you through the experience of knowing Him. God Himself is faith; He is the system of beliefs that we submit to. We also note that He challenged us to prove Him because He is always present and in every situation. I will focus on a theme: Now Faith Is.

The Burden of Proof

When the Lord placed this in my spirit, I was reluctant to embrace it because of the word *burden*, but there was a continued thought that I was not able to forget. With thought, I began to understand: We know according to the Word of God that once we are in God, He takes our burden and our cares and casts them on Himself.

> Come to me, all you that labor and are heavy laden, and
> I will give you rest.
>
> Take my yoke on you, and learn of me; for I am meek
> and lowly in heart: and you shall find rest to your souls.
>
> For my yoke is easy, and my burden is light. (Matthew
> 11:28–30)

So burden, as I understand it, can be compared to a legal principle. I consulted Pastor Dave (my husband) to explain. Following is Pastor Dave's explanation of burden of proof:

> The rule is that the person who avers must prove his or
> her assertions. When the burden of proof is on you, know
> the following:

1. At the highest standard is beyond reasonable doubt. When proving or attempting to put a case of innocence, the evidence must be beyond reasonable doubt.

2. On the balance of probabilities or preponderance of doubt (lowest standard), if doubt arises or if the person is asserting anything and there is still some doubt, then the accused should go free.

So, God wants us to prove Him by looking at the facts. Look at the records thus far; He is God. Everything that you and I would have learned from Genesis to Revelation is all God. So, God is saying the scripture is a proven theory. It is a system of ideas and axioms that have been proven and proven again about the existence of Creation and have been found to be true. In our case He is saying that if we have proven Him at the highest level of the law, beyond a reasonable doubt, then the burden is on us to establish Him as who He is. But just on the chance that He hasn't established Himself in our lives, then He would not be who He claims to be. On the other hand, if He only showed up but once or according to us in some small way, then the burden is on us to prove Him again because we have the proof—regardless how small it is.

So, I present to you the theorem as verified in the lives of saints present and those gone before. Even those without a household of faith can say truthfully it is so. The theorem is: the God of the universe is true to His Word.

We are still in the book of Hebrews chapter 11, and still in the first verse. We read, "Now faith is the substance of things hoped for, the evidence of things not seen."

Substance, a noun, means (1) a particular kind of matter with uniform properties and (2) the real physical matter of which a person or thing consists and that has a tangible, solid presence.

Hope is a feeling of expectation and a desire for a particular thing to happen.

Evidence, broadly construed, is anything presented in support of an assertion. This support may be strong or weak. The strongest type of evidence is that which provides direct proof of the truth of an assertion.

God is saying that He is the matter, He is our aspiration, and He is the support of any argument or challenge.

For by him were all things created, that are in heaven, and that are in earth, visible and invisible, whether they be thrones, or dominions, or principalities, or powers: all things were created by him, and for him:

And he is before all things, and by him all things consist.

And he is the head of the body, the church: who is the beginning, the firstborn from the dead; that in all things he might have the preeminence.

For it pleased the Father that in him should all fullness dwell;

And, having made peace through the blood of his cross, by him to reconcile all things to himself; by him, I say, whether they be things in earth, or things in heaven. (Colossians 1:16–20)

The same was in the beginning with God.

All things were made by him; and without him was not any thing made that was made.

In him was life; and the life was the light of men. (John 1:1–3)

To verify His existence, therefore, we must be in Him. It is from this position inside Him that we can know Him and that all reasonable doubt can be erased. To be in Him means simply to submit to His will by repentance. This means personal reformation and application of the Word. We know then that faith comes by hearing, hearing the Word of God, for He is His Word.

I'll share with you an insight into knowing God that He revealed to me:

The length of prayer or how hard we pray has nothing to do with making sure God hears our prayer. He hears us from the first time. As a matter of fact, He knows the very thoughts and intentions of our hearts. But the burden is on us to settle within ourselves that He is God and He can and will do what His Word documents.

For someone to document who they are in writing and then, in the same text, challenge anyone who reads it to prove Him must be infallible, to say the least, and confident. God is. He exists without variation. The time we take in prayer is because we need the experience to align our faith with the Word of God. He is His Word.

So, we see:

> But without faith it is impossible to please him: for he that comes to God must believe that he is, and that he is a rewarder of them that diligently seek him. (Hebrews 11:6)

"Coming to God" literally means arriving at that place where our bodies, minds, and spirits accept all of God, rejecting none of Him. It means to completely take Him at His Word wholeheartedly, doubting nothing. God would have us to understand that the burden of proof is on us.

We then have to affirm His assertions that He is God, He is a Deliverer, He is a Healer, He is a Friend, He is a Provider, and He is a Sustainer. The level of faith has gone up before Him and suggests to Him that we, the people of God, have not accepted that His Word is true. It seems that we doubt His ability to do what He says He will.

In response, God presents His Word. He submits to our legal system. He allows Himself to be tried at human discretion. He makes His godly status vulnerable to our legal discourse. And so, forgetting the highest level of burden of proof, beyond reasonable doubt, let us look at the lowest level, on the balance of probability, to establish our case. So here in our midst, the King of kings and Lord of lords is accused of not being God, that is, not delivering as He said He would, not healing as He said He would.

At the very lowest level, if we have seen Him come through in any instance, God desires, then that we trust Him. Because we would have had prayers answered, the charges may have some level of doubt but because of God's record of being present for His people, a strong case to prove His innocence. Let's take Him up on this challenge now.

"I call the court convening between earth and heaven in session now. I command angels and the host of heaven to join in tonight with the congregation of the saints, and the reader, to verify the truth of all godly assertions. I command the King of kings to reveal Himself this moment to His people. May Truth be established. Amen."

*   *   *

Prayer

Father, I have doubted You. I have doubted Your existence of supremacy and Your ability to deliver, to heal, and to empower. Please forgive me. And as I see You for who You are, let me experience a new life of faith in You. Grant me the privilege to see You move in the lives of others and in my life as a result of this experience today.

Amen.

Declaration

I declare this day that I will walk continuously in the knowledge of the Christ. I will not only fellowship with Him but also testify of His existence. I declare that my daily witness, my conversation, my ministry, my work, and my play will prove the God is alive and well. I confess that God is good. He always is. He is righteous and altogether lovely. There is no failure in God. He alone is God, and there is no other!

CHAPTER 13
Express Gratitude

Enter into his gates with thanksgiving, and into his courts with praise: be thankful to him, and bless his name.

—Psalm 100:4

An Expression of Gratitude

It is very important to pause sometimes and, in a unique or accepted manner, convey a message of appreciation to those who have offered words of encouragement or help in any way. People are meant to communicate with each other, and such interactions expressing extending of assistance, greeting, affection, respect, sympathy, apology, acceptance, or gratefulness, in addition to so many other possibilities, make life enjoyable and fulfilling. Whether we admit it or not, we enjoy social interaction. We are wired to give and receive. This is the godly plan.

As we enjoy and participate in such exchanges without even knowing in most instances, how much more so our porter? Are we not made in His image and His likeness?

> So God created man in his own image, in the image of
> God created he him; male and female created he them.
> (Genesis 1:27)

I believe that we have the characteristics of a very sociable God. He invites us speak to Him daily. As, in any earthly family, we do not ask for things throughout our conversation with a parent, we would not spend an entire prayer session petitioning. Worse, we will not be petitioning every time we pray. Experience tells us that most people are either motivated to do good or appreciate responses of gratitude for any level of kindness they show. God is like this. He enjoys our individual expressions, reciting in sincerity our appreciation for His grace, favor, healing, and presence in our lives.

The expression of gratitude is of significance to our purpose. We were created to adore the Lord.

> And the four beasts had each of them six wings about him;
> and they were full of eyes within: and they rest not day
> and night, saying, Holy, holy, holy, Lord God Almighty,
> which was, and is, and is to come.

And when those beasts give glory and honor and thanks to him that sat on the throne, who lives for ever and ever,

The four and twenty elders fall down before him that sat on the throne, and worship him that lives for ever and ever, and cast their crowns before the throne, saying,

You are worthy, O Lord, to receive glory and honor and power: for you have created all things, and for your pleasure they are and were created. (Revelation 4:8–11)

Give Thanks for Where You Are

Give thanks for where God brought you from and doe the victories He has won for you. Take time to itemize everything, saying thanks. This exercise will allow you to have a clear map of your faith journey. At each step, look back to calculate and evaluate your faith and God's faithfulness. See how He did it, and say thanks. This will motivate you to trust Him more.

Oftentimes, because we are determined to reap ultimate results, we forget to pause to evaluate our progress. When we pause, we are able to see God's work in our lives. We can see His progressive guidance in increments. It may not and will never be our destination with the nature of the God we serve.

Saying thank you is, again, an affirmation of faith. We are admitting that we did not arrive at any point in life by our own merit or insight. We are acknowledging God's intervention and power to change our circumstances.

Sometimes progress may be limited or may not occur at all. This may call for a deeper look into progress. Perhaps your ability to persevere has grown. Maybe your emotional response to hard circumstances has changed. Maybe it is the way you think as a result of experiences you've had or how you process survival. Sometimes our value systems have been completely destroyed and we find ourselves beginning to think as God thinks. As change continues, we desire godly things. So, this is marked progress. It is worth praising Him for. This is the change that introduces the possibility for miracles.

It Is God's Will

The Lord created all things for His pleasure. We were created to give God glory. This is by design. God responds to our admiration. He expects it and looks forward to hearing our responses. He is good by nature and expects His creation not only to exude His characteristics but also to communicate with Him in His intended way. He gives us His best and loves us beyond measure. In return, He expects the same from us.

> In every thing give thanks: for this is the will of God in Christ Jesus concerning you. (1 Thessalonians 5:18)

Praise Invites God's Presence

The nature of God is such that He enjoys life. He is life. He encourages celebrations and the appreciation of those around us. This is why we are expected to be stewards, to fellowship regularly, to sing praises, and to encourage each other.

One writer of the Psalms described God as holy. This is a characteristic that distinguishes the Lord as supreme, uncompared and unmatched by any other God. It also separates us from God in the sense that we are not able to attain such a state of purity on our own merit. However, the following verse indicates that in spite of this vast difference, God has chosen humankind to communicate with. When we communicate our appreciation for His merciful kindness toward us, it creates an environment for Him to communicate and enjoy being with us. As we praise Him, we are honored with His response, His presence. His presence is to hear and respond to the requests of His people.

> But you are holy, O you that inhabit the praises of Israel. (Psalm 22:3)

Prayer and praise are of great value to God. There is a procedure for handling the prayers of the saints. These prayers are collected in vessels that are held by the twenty-four elders. Believe it or not, prayer has an order.

And when he had taken the book, the four beasts and four and twenty elders fell down before the Lamb, having every one of them harps, and golden vials full of odors, which are the prayers of saints. (Revelation 5:8)

And the smoke of the incense, which came with the prayers of the saints, ascended up before God out of the angel's hand. (Revelation 8:4)

Praise Produces Miracles

Paul and Silas demonstrated the power of prayer while they were imprisoned in a jail. They did not remain in a surrendered mindset but instead loudly gave God glory. They did not accept the actions of the guards to be final. They obviously had their faith in another, greater than the authorities who had sentenced them.

They cried out in petition and worship, and God heard them. His response to Paul and Silas was immediate. The scripture gave the time to be about midnight. They should have been sleeping by our modern practices, but they saw a greater need. When God responded, the prison shook, and this created fear. What accompanied the shaking was of greater significance: the chains fell off, and the gates were opened automatically. The guards feared for their lives; the power of God interrupted the order they had established. Paul and Silas were freed. There was also a witness among the unbelieving guards of the faithfulness of the Lord.

And at midnight Paul and Silas prayed, and sang praises to God: and the prisoners heard them.

And suddenly there was a great earthquake, so that the foundations of the prison were shaken: and immediately all the doors were opened, and every one's bands were loosed.

And the keeper of the prison awaking out of his sleep, and seeing the prison doors open, he drew out his sword, and would have killed himself, supposing that the prisoners had been fled.

But Paul cried with a loud voice, saying, Do yourself no harm: for we are all here.

Then he called for a light, and sprang in, and came trembling, and fell down before Paul and Silas,

And brought them out, and said, Sirs, what must I do to be saved?

And they said, Believe on the Lord Jesus Christ, and you shall be saved, and your house.

And they spoke to him the word of the Lord, and to all that were in his house.

And he took them the same hour of the night, and washed their stripes; and was baptized, he and all his, straightway.

And when he had brought them into his house, he set meat before them, and rejoiced, believing in God with all his house. (Acts 16:25–34)

The Walls of Jericho

When the people of God cry out to Him, there is no limitations to God's response. He chooses how He desires to manifest Himself. With Paul and Silas, they cried out and He loosed their chains and liberated them from the jail. In the case of Jericho, He took a different approach to fighting for His people. He gave them instructions. The specific instruction was to allow the children of Israel to witness firsthand how God defies nature at His pleasure. All the laws of science were challenged by the shout of an obedient people.

Now Jericho was straightly shut up because of the children of Israel: none went out, and none came in.

And the Lord said to Joshua, See, I have given into your hand Jericho, and the king thereof, and the mighty men of valor.

And you shall compass the city, all you men of war, and go round about the city once. Thus shall you do six days.

And seven priests shall bear before the ark seven trumpets of rams' horns: and the seventh day you shall compass the city seven times, and the priests shall blow with the trumpets.

And it shall come to pass, that when they make a long blast with the ram's horn, and when you hear the sound of the trumpet, all the people shall shout with a great shout; and the wall of the city shall fall down flat, and the people shall ascend up every man straight before him. …

And Joshua the son of Nun called the priests, and said to them, Take up the ark of the covenant, and let seven priests bear seven trumpets of rams' horns before the ark of the Lord.

And he said to the people, Pass on, and compass the city, and let him that is armed pass on before the ark of the Lord.

And it came to pass, when Joshua had spoken to the people, that the seven priests bearing the seven trumpets of rams' horns passed on before the Lord, and blew with the trumpets: and the ark of the covenant of the Lord followed them.

And the armed men went before the priests that blew with the trumpets, and the rear guard came after the ark, the priests going on, and blowing with the trumpets.

And Joshua had commanded the people, saying, You shall not shout, nor make any noise with your voice, neither shall any word proceed out of your mouth, until the day I bid you shout; then shall you shout.

So the ark of the Lord compassed the city, going about it once: and they came into the camp, and lodged in the camp.

And Joshua rose early in the morning, and the priests took up the ark of the Lord. (Joshua 6:1–5; 6–12)

Praise Seals Our Miracles

When we pray, we see results. Sometimes these results are permanent, and other times they seem to be lost without any understanding as to why. The story of the ten lepers may shed some light on some reason why. This may not be the answer to all situations, but for a number of cases this is true. This story suggests strongly that the majority of people asking for divine assistance are not grateful.

There were ten men with leprosy who cried out to Jesus. The Lord Jesus, without bias, healed all ten of them. It follows by the action of the nine lepers that they seemed to have assumed a right to the healing. The majority continued on their way. The nine, according to the scripture, did not return to Jesus. There was just the one who returned to Jesus and expressed his gratitude.

It was the act of returning to give God glory that made this man whole as Jesus said. This act was called faith. By faith we are justified. The grateful man was healed and blessed by His single act. He was alone, but he was right to do as he did—and Jesus blessed him accordingly.

And it came to pass, as he went to Jerusalem, that he passed through the middle of Samaria and Galilee.

And as he entered into a certain village, there met him ten men that were lepers, which stood afar off:

And they lifted up their voices, and said, Jesus, Master, have mercy on us.

And when he saw them, he said to them, Go show yourselves to the priests. And it came to pass, that, as they went, they were cleansed.

And one of them, when he saw that he was healed, turned back, and with a loud voice glorified God,

And fell down on his face at his feet, giving him thanks: and he was a Samaritan.

And Jesus answering said, Were there not ten cleansed? but where are the nine?

There are not found that returned to give glory to God, save this stranger.

And he said to him, Arise, go your way: your faith has made you whole. (Luke 17:11–19)

Expressions of Gratitude Give a Lasting Remembrance

In this era of the church, there was a literal obedience to the command to be separate from sinners. By the story of the Samaritan, we know that there was a division among races and among classes in Jewish society. Likewise, a woman in the presence of distinguished man, by this account, was frowned on.

But this woman had more than her gender against her. It was more so her character. She was known in the community to have had several husbands. It is said the man she remained with was not her husband. In the religious community, she was an outcast. Her gestures of kindness were not appreciated by Jesus's hosts simply because of her reputation. Jesus, on the other hand, looked beyond her lifestyle and saw the repentance of her heart. He, in turn, defended her and blessed her for her adoration.

> And one of the Pharisees desired him that he would eat with him. And he went into the Pharisee's house, and sat down to meat.
>
> And, behold, a woman in the city, which was a sinner, when she knew that Jesus sat at meat in the Pharisee's house, brought an alabaster box of ointment,
>
> And stood at his feet behind him weeping, and began to wash his feet with tears, and did wipe them with the hairs of her head, and kissed his feet, and anointed them with the ointment.
>
> Now when the Pharisee which had bidden him saw it, he spoke within himself, saying, This man, if he were a prophet, would have known who and what manner of woman this is that touches him: for she is a sinner.
>
> And Jesus answering said to him, Simon, I have somewhat to say to you. And he said, Master, say on.
>
> There was a certain creditor which had two debtors: the one owed five hundred pence, and the other fifty.
>
> And when they had nothing to pay, he frankly forgave them both. Tell me therefore, which of them will love him most?
>
> Simon answered and said, I suppose that he, to whom he forgave most. And he said to him, You have rightly judged.

And he turned to the woman, and said to Simon, See you this woman? I entered into your house, you gave me no water for my feet: but she has washed my feet with tears, and wiped them with the hairs of her head.

You gave me no kiss: but this woman since the time I came in has not ceased to kiss my feet.

My head with oil you did not anoint: but this woman has anointed my feet with ointment.

Why I say to you, Her sins, which are many, are forgiven; for she loved much: but to whom little is forgiven, the same loves little.

And he said to her, Your sins are forgiven.

And they that sat at meat with him began to say within themselves, Who is this that forgives sins also?

And he said to the woman, Your faith has saved you; go in peace. (Luke 7:36–50)

*   *   *

Prayer

Father, I give You thanks and praise for being a faithful God. I thank You for the many times that You have brought me out of challenges that I never thought I would have overcome. Thank You for Your wisdom, Your grace, Your mercies, Your kindness, and Your favor. Had it not been for You, I don't know where I would be.

I wish to pause to acknowledge Your guidance every step of the way. Thank You for Your strength, wisdom, and instructions. Without them I would have failed, but You carried me through. For this I still have hope. I thank You. I thank You for a brighter tomorrow, and I thank You for Your presence in yesterday's challenges.

Thank You, Father.

Amen.

Declaration

I will continuously bless the Lord for He is good and His mercies endure forever. I have seen the hand of God in many situations, and I know He will deliver me. My lips will always have praises flowing from them because I know He will always be present when I praise.

Mighty is the Lord, worthy of all praise and glory. When I cry, the Lord hears and delivers me out of not one, or two, or three, but all my troubles. So I set myself to rejoice today and always because God is faithful. I've seen it with my own eyes.

As I count the things I've endured, the favors I have received, I declare it was God alone, so I bless You today, Father. I will bless You tomorrow, and I will bless You always.

Hallelujah!

CHAPTER 14
Expect Great Things

Now to him that is able to do exceeding abundantly above all that we ask or think, according to the power that works in us.

—Ephesians 3:20

I remember experiencing a very challenging time in my life. I was losing everything and was fighting in every area of my life. The enemy did not spare hardship on any side. It seems as though the design was to layer the problems as I tried to solve them. No matter how I tried to repair any of the challenging problems, the situation became worse as I lost even more money and had even worse relationships, the list of things going wrong growing daily.

After years of fighting, I finally gave up. I walked away from everything. I left everything behind. I said nothing. I left people to assume what they would. I simply kept praying. I believe God to be a Deliverer. Not my acquaintances. I believe God.

It was my faith in God's ability to deliver that kept me sane. I was deep in dept. People were celebrating my failures. They were expecting my failure and began anticipating it. Some even seemed to be praying for it. Worse yet, they seemed to be wishing for even further devastation. They knew that I had failed miserably and that there was no return. This was the one point that both my critics and I seemed to agree on.

I walked away from everything without telling anyone too many details, if anything at all. I felt defeated, yet I continued to pray. It is through prayer that I felt God's hand keeping me. One day the Lord placed a statement into my spirit that was so profound that it completely lifted the gloom I was feeling. The words were "Consented impossibilities become reality when driven by the catalyst of passion."

I instantly understood what it meant and began quoting it to my children and other people. I made it my WhatsApp status and appended it to my emails. My ability to process failure was being revolutionized by one divine thought. There was a solution to my dilemma: passion.

Passion to overcome my circumstances was the ingredient to speed up the change, encourage change, and facilitate it. The question then was "Is my passion for what I have lost stronger than the magnitude of my loss?" For change it had to be. Otherwise failure would be permanent. Passion or desire keeps expectations high. Expectation or hope increases the possibility of dreams becoming reality.

We Have This Hope

Wherein God, willing more abundantly to show to the heirs of promise the immutability of his counsel, confirmed it by an oath:

That by two immutable things, in which it was impossible for God to lie, we might have a strong consolation, who have fled for refuge to lay hold on the hope set before us:

Which hope we have as an anchor of the soul, both sure and steadfast, and which enters into that within the veil;

—Hebrews 6:17–19

And hope makes not ashamed; because the love of God is shed abroad in our hearts by the Holy Ghost which is given to us.

—Romans 5:5

But we have this treasure in earthen vessels, that the excellency of the power may be of God, and not of us.

—2 Corinthians 4:7

The foregoing three scriptures tell us one thing very clearly. After reading, there is no doubt where our hope should rest. These scriptures all document the fact that God has the power to break through our present circumstance by His unchanging character and not by our strength or ability. So the possibility of embarrassment is nonexistent. We have eliminated the human factor and have sought to invoke the assistance of a God who is more than enough. This hope, this confidence, is in the authority of the Godhead, not mortal humankind.

We know that God cannot lie. Because of this attribute of His, we can conclude that His promises in His Word are not only true but also enduring. We are further advised in the scriptures that God does not change:

Jesus Christ the same yesterday, and to day, and for ever.
(Hebrews 13:8)

What God says today will hold for eternity. This in the confidence we
have in His character. We are guided by the scriptures and have become
strengthened in our faith because of the testimony of other saints. As they
share their stories of triumph through belief in the record in the scriptures,
they affirm the validity of the enduring power of an all-powerful God.
This is what keeps our faith alive.

As we read in the previous chapter, Paul and Silas saw the manifestation
of God's power to deliver. The sight of it by prisoners made them believe.
This feat even overwhelmed the jailers. This event was a powerful testimony
to the truth of the hope in the gospel. It proved that if we call on the Lord,
He will deliver.

For whoever shall call on the name of the Lord shall be
saved. (Romans 10:13)

Jesus answered them, I told you, and you believed not: the
works that I do in my Father's name, they bear witness
of me.

But you believe not, because you are not of my sheep, as
I said to you. (John 10:25–26)

The authorities were intimidated by it. The proof with evidence was
enough to convert the community to Christianity. I believe this is why the
scripture says that tongues are a sign for those without the faith.

Why tongues are for a sign, not to them that believe, but
to them that believe not: but prophesying serves not for
them that believe not, but for them which believe.

If therefore the whole church be come together into one
place, and all speak with tongues, and there come in those
that are unlearned, or unbelievers, will they not say that
you are mad?

> But if all prophesy, and there come in one that believes
> not, or one unlearned, he is convinced of all, he is judged
> of all. (1 Corinthians 14:22–24 KJV)

When someone hears of a belief system, especially one as demonstrative as Christianity, the question might arise as to the validity of the parables and stories in the Bible. The picture painted of the Israelites crossing on dry land and the water drowning their pursuers is an elaborate portrayal of nature's defiance of natural laws.

But yet we believe and hear testimonies of Christians speaking of other modern experiences of the laws of nature being breached for the facilitation of God's divine will. The participants in such miracles can testify that they had read one or more such biblical stories and that this was their motivation. Knowing that it happened before established a precedent and activated the faith to see the impossible.

God of Our Fathers

> And said, O Lord God of our fathers, are not you God
> in heaven? and rule not you over all the kingdoms of the
> heathen? and in your hand is there not power and might,
> so that none is able to withstand you?
>
> —2 Chronicles 20:6

Accompanying precedents is the relationship of the recipients with the Lord. This provides a great hope. For many saints, covenants were formed with the Lord that extended to generations. These covenants have as a clause the divine presence of God throughout the generations of their bloodline. And so, children, grandchildren, and generations to follow may gain God's attention by reminding Him of His covenant with their forebears. For us, our parents, grandparents, or great-grandparents may have made a covenant, and so we might remind God of their faithfulness to Him.

This does not exempt us from doing what is right. It merely gives us an invitation to challenge God to perform the miracle that we need. In particular, if He had done similar works for our family member, we would petition the

Lord, reminding Him of His covenant and expecting that He will extend His favor to us as well. We can expect with great hope that He will consider us because He had demonstrated His ability before. This provides the faith we need to be consistent in prayer. It does not limit Him to such ability.

Removing the Limits

God cannot be contained. He is definitely not limited by our ability to perceive Him. Hebrews 6:17–19 reminds us that as much as we can imagine, He will be more than that. Whatever we can begin to think possible excels those possibilities by far. Our God thinks higher, and His ways supersede those of His creation.

There is therefore no way we can ask too much of Him or ask something impossible for Him to perform. He is life, and when we ask for anything, literally we are asking Him for some aspect of Himself. That is easy to give; the consideration should be, and always is, if we can handle it.

* * *

Prayer

Lord, thank You for Your kindness. Your mercies have been new each morning. You have proven Your Word is true in everything that I have presented to You, even the things that I have failed to mention. You revealed Your power to deliver in each one. Thank You. Thank You for the abundant grace You poured out on me. Without it I would not have overcome.

Father, I look to You because You are able to do exceedingly, abundantly above what I might ask or even imagine. I look to You because You are more than able to see me through and to enlarge my territory. You have the power to subdue every opposition to Your will for me, the power to promote, to bless, to transform, or to terminate.

I know that You wish that I would prosper, so I look to You to keep me and uplift me. I'm expecting You to do so according to Your Word. I thank You for it.

Amen.

Declaration

I am the head and not the tail.

I am above only and not beneath.

I am the righteousness of God in Christ Jesus and, therefore, a joint heir with Christ.

I am lacking nothing because everything to live godly I have already.

I have a righteous God who defends me and seeks to give me His best.

Because of His love for me, my cup overflows. It is my spiritual right.

Each day I look for this manifestation.

I expect it.

I praise for it.

I command it.

By His mercies, I will possess it!

In the name of Jesus.

CHAPTER 15
Now Encourage Someone

And such as do wickedly against the covenant shall he corrupt by flatteries: but the people that do know their God shall be strong, and do exploits.

—Daniel 11:32

The kingdom of God is structured so that every member of the community of believers has an organized part to play in its advancement. There is order and structured networking divinely designed for the advancement of the kingdom. The way in which the Lord created us was to ensure that there was a continuous interaction. Look at the way He created Eve, from Adam's rib. This implies that there is something in us that comes from Someone and that this thing would make that Someone complete. So, we need to hang around. We might not return or give up the thing because we need this thing too. It defines us and may ultimately determine our existence. However, it can be shared, effectively reaching others and transforming their lives for God's glory.

As we share, we will find that we do not understand this attribute better, but we grow and become even more effective. We have an enriched and fulfilling life. So, giving is designed for empowerment, not to feed greed. Adam gave his rib because God used this to give life to Eve. Consequently, the life that Eve received was what Adam needed. The life offered Adam companionship. Eve had an opportunity to work with Adam and name all living things as they dominated earth. Life also allowed them to enjoy children and ultimately nations.

A shared gift has a way of multiplying for the benefit of the community. There is wisdom in its use that determines how far-reaching it will be. Our communal effort brings out and matures our gifting, whether the experience is favorable or not. This shared communication and interaction is a learning experience. It is a becoming, a development encounter. We must apply the scripture thoroughly to the way we respond to challenges that may arise and to the application and planning of any process we might undertake.

We are never any less enriched to share who we are with others. Our essence is the treasure of spiritual empowerment. When we identify with our brothers and sisters in Christ, we know that we have the same spirit. We know this is common and binding. However, to get to the next level, the next encounter, we must add to our kinspeople that thing which they need. This will serve as fuel and maybe as a turbo charge. For us, we will see the need for this attribute clearly. However, this attribute may or may not be the thing that the brother or sister is looking for.

The approach to release this thing should be prayed about throughout and organized very well in love. Any wrong decision, poor choice of words, or negative act may be perceived in the wrong light. These mistakes or poor judgments may be long-lasting and damaging to the individual believer. So caution or consent would be wise. If there is consent or, even better, an invitation, then wisdom is still needed, but there is greater freedom to share because of the willingness. Our care for each other will determine how far we reach, how we mature, how effective our gifting is. While the Lord encourages each believer to be strong and work out his or her own salvation, He insists that we are one.

We Are One Body
We are grafted in to the body!

We are to understand that spiritually, we are united. The Lord has purposed that there is a connecting factor. This will draw us whether we like it or not. As a result, we are expected to function temporally as though we are united. This connection transcends race, nationality, status, and any other determinant. It ignores our presumptions and establishes a truth, the truth of the mysteries of Christ.

Justin Barrett, PhD, in his March 5, 2013, article "Are We Born Believing in God?", asserts that the studies conducted by Andrew Meltzoff and M. Keith Moore on newborn babies and their ability to recognize familiar faces and mimic them, in addition to having innate behavior, show only one of several subsystems relating to the human mind. These, he said, are normal and result from the constraints in our environment, along with inborn behavior. Further, he asserts that these subsystems ultimately influence our religious beliefs. The studies affirm the scriptures:

- We have behaviors that are a part of our makeup.

    Simon Peter, a servant and an apostle of Jesus Christ, to them that have obtained like precious faith with us through the righteousness of God and our Savior Jesus Christ:

Grace and peace be multiplied to you through the knowledge of God, and of Jesus our Lord,

According as his divine power has given to us all things that pertain to life and godliness, through the knowledge of him that has called us to glory and virtue. (2 Peter 1:3)

These subsystems lead us to identify with others and connect with God.

Having predestinated us to the adoption of children by Jesus Christ to himself, according to the good pleasure of his will,

To the praise of the glory of his grace, wherein he has made us accepted in the beloved.

In whom we have redemption through his blood, the forgiveness of sins, according to the riches of his grace;

Wherein he has abounded toward us in all wisdom and prudence;

Having made known to us the mystery of his will, according to his good pleasure which he has purposed in himself:

That in the dispensation of the fullness of times he might gather together in one all things in Christ, both which are in heaven, and which are on earth; even in him:

In whom also we have obtained an inheritance, being predestinated according to the purpose of him who works all things after the counsel of his own will:

That we should be to the praise of his glory, who first trusted in Christ. (Ephesians 1:5–12)

Why I also, after I heard of your faith in the Lord Jesus, and love to all the saints,

Cease not to give thanks for you, making mention of you in my prayers. (Ephesians 4:15–16)

So, we see that in interacting with others, understanding how they do things, and even mimicking them, we learn and find our way to God. Therefore, we can conclude that it is unhealthy to have bad relationships. These relations will prevent us from discovering who we are, limit our potential, and hinder the process of entering into a meaningful relationship with God—and ultimately, we will live a life without purpose.

Division Brings Destruction and Delay

When we divide, someone will not get what is needed to overcome. We are interdependent. Paul alluded to this truth several times in his writings. He was grateful for the care of the saints.

But I rejoiced in the Lord greatly, that now at the last your care of me has flourished again; wherein you were also careful, but you lacked opportunity. (Philippians 4:10)

He insisted that they cause him to find joy in what they do.

And I wrote this same to you, lest, when I came, I should have sorrow from them of whom I ought to rejoice; having confidence in you all, that my joy is the joy of you all. (2 Corinthians 2:3)

We are asked to be stewards. It is by design that we care for each other.

As every man has received the gift, even so minister the same one to another, as good stewards of the manifold grace of God. (1 Peter 4:10)

Moreover it is required in stewards, that a man be found faithful. (1 Corinthians 4:2)

This is our spiritual mandate. He or she who is spiritual should restore those who fall. So, to leave a brother or sister alone is not the will of God. I have noticed a turn to the following:

- materialism,
- social rejection of those not of our status, and
- the use of implying little messages in hopes that the wise will pick up these hints and find their way. If not, it's not our responsibility.

These are all confirmation that we are in the last days—a great reason to stop them immediately. Where is the expression of love in any of these? Without love, our efforts are in vain. When we divorce ourselves from walking in love with our brother and sister, we have separated ourselves from God. This action cries out, saying that He is not in us. God is love. A lack of love in fellowship, stewardship, ministry, and living is an absence of God.

Beloved, let us love one another: for love is of God; and every one that loves is born of God, and knows God.

He that loves not knows not God; for God is love. (1 John 4:7–8)

Though I speak with the tongues of men and of angels, and have not charity, I am become as sounding brass, or a tinkling cymbal.

And though I have the gift of prophecy, and understand all mysteries, and all knowledge; and though I have all faith, so that I could remove mountains, and have not charity, I am nothing.

And though I bestow all my goods to feed the poor, and though I give my body to be burned, and have not charity, it profits me nothing.

Charity suffers long, and is kind; charity envies not; charity brags not itself, is not puffed up,

Does not behave itself unseemly, seeks not her own, is not easily provoked, thinks no evil;

Rejoices not in iniquity, but rejoices in the truth;

Bears all things, believes all things, hopes all things, endures all things.

Charity never fails: but whether there be prophecies, they shall fail; whether there be tongues, they shall cease; whether there be knowledge, it shall vanish away.

For we know in part, and we prophesy in part.

But when that which is perfect is come, then that which is in part shall be done away.

When I was a child, I spoke as a child, I understood as a child, I thought as a child: but when I became a man, I put away childish things.

For now we see through a glass, darkly; but then face to face: now I know in part; but then shall I know even as also I am known.

And now stays faith, hope, charity, these three; but the greatest of these is charity. (1 Corinthians 13)

In giving, it abounds to our reward.

> Give, and it shall be given to you; good measure, pressed down, and shaken together, and running over, shall men give into your bosom. For with the same measure that you mete with it shall be measured to you again. (Luke 6:38)

> Who has believed our report? and to whom is the arm of the Lord revealed?

> For he shall grow up before him as a tender plant, and as a root out of a dry ground: he has no form nor comeliness; and when we shall see him, there is no beauty that we should desire him.

> He is despised and rejected of men; a man of sorrows, and acquainted with grief: and we hid as it were our faces from him; he was despised, and we esteemed him not.

> Surely he has borne our griefs, and carried our sorrows: yet we did esteem him stricken, smitten of God, and afflicted.

> But he was wounded for our transgressions, he was bruised for our iniquities: the chastisement of our peace was on him; and with his stripes we are healed.

> All we like sheep have gone astray; we have turned every one to his own way; and the Lord has laid on him the iniquity of us all.

> He was oppressed, and he was afflicted, yet he opened not his mouth: he is brought as a lamb to the slaughter, and as a sheep before her shearers is dumb, so he opens not his mouth.

> He was taken from prison and from judgment: and who shall declare his generation? for he was cut off out of the

land of the living: for the transgression of my people was he stricken.

And he made his grave with the wicked, and with the rich in his death; because he had done no violence, neither was any deceit in his mouth.

Yet it pleased the Lord to bruise him; he has put him to grief: when you shall make his soul an offering for sin, he shall see his seed, he shall prolong his days, and the pleasure of the Lord shall prosper in his hand.

He shall see of the travail of his soul, and shall be satisfied: by his knowledge shall my righteous servant justify many; for he shall bear their iniquities.

Therefore will I divide him a portion with the great, and he shall divide the spoil with the strong; because he has poured out his soul to death: and he was numbered with the transgressors; and he bore the sin of many, and made intercession for the transgressors. (Isaiah 53)

How Do We Encourage Others?

Share Scriptures

The Word of God is therapy itself. It not only gives instructions but also provides comfort. Hearing God's Word specific to a given situation will awaken hope and perhaps inspire a new outlook. Try quoting a few scriptures of God's promises. Simply reminding a loved one of his or her position in God can be enough.

Be There—Call, Spend Time, Encourage

There is great motivation from just having a well-wisher present. Oftentimes it costs little, if anything, to visit someone who may be experiencing a challenging time just to talk. There may not be a need for the individual to vent. The person may simply enjoy an everyday conversation that distracts him or her from what the person might be facing. Some people enjoy a laugh to lighten their spirits. Just one outburst can change someone's entire course in life.

On the other hand, motivating words will spark a sense of confidence. Offer advice based on experience or knowledge. Sometimes a smile is a greater motivator than expected.

Do—Help Physically

Perhaps you are all too familiar with what someone else might be experiencing. You might feel God's Spirit leading you to assist. You can begin by talking, but why not write a plan and, in phases, work toward making the solution a reality? You may not need to work from start to finish; perhaps a perfectly good plan may already be in place.

In this instance, see how you can provide support. Consider offering any skill you may have to make the transition easier. You may have human or material resources. This is important. It is in giving that we receive.

> And to know the love of Christ, which passes knowledge,
> that you might be filled with all the fullness of God.
> (Ephesians 3:19)

* * *

Prayer

> I plunge [insert here whatever the challenge is—that is,
> name it] under the blood, and I command forth [insert the
> name of the intended victory], according to God's Word,
> [insert scripture reference here] in the name of Jesus.

Throwing the oil to the ground, say, "I command that the earth open and release a miracle!"

Clapping, shout, "Glory, hallelujah!"

This indicates complete confidence in God's ability to deliver, along with approval of and appreciation for His intervention. It is a faith-release exercise. Clapping is a sign of triumph.

Declaration

My life is a record of God's goodness and faithfulness. I declare that He has been good. I shall not remain silent. I will echo aloud His benefits so that believers and sinners will submit to His leadership and trust His Word.

CHAPTER 16
Conclusion

I, like many saints, have had countless battles. These seem to have increased instead of decreased. I am sure many of us have had prophecies stating how God will deliver. For some of these, we have seen immediate manifestations, but for the greater part, as with Abraham, we have had to wait. This wait, if in God, will never kill us but will equip us to be examples and ministers of God to promote His gospel on the earth. I have experienced this prolonged wait. I prayed, fasted, sowed, worked in ministry, shut up, and put up with a whole lot of expecting the miraculous, but still I had to wait. Waiting may hurt, but when we wait with the knowledge of the authority of Christ and the true nature of the Lord, we will not be discouraged but full of hope. The process beautifies the spirit of humankind. It denies the flesh of immediate gratification and directs our attention to Jesus Christ.

The more we address the challenge, the better acquainted we become with the Lord. We learn how He thinks, how He responds, and how much He really cares. He gives specific instructions, and we, after following these and seeing the effect, grow and increase in confidence.

God Is Glorified

I thought to share some testimonies to further encourage everyone who reads *Releasing the Overcomer's Anointing*. It is not an easy task to follow the path of righteousness, but the reward is glorious. As the scripture says, we may cry for a while, but there is no doubt that we will return with a smile and a harvest. I have raised three children, and that experience was not the easiest. They were and are three personalities, three distinctly different temperaments, with their diverse opinions on most things. Thankfully, the common ground has been our faith. They know intimately my challenges and my strengths and were a part of them all as we looked to God for His guidance. So, I asked my family to share their thoughts as a testament to what God can and will do if we trust Him.

Testimonies

Growing up in a household that is committed to Christianity and God is one of the most fundamental things people need in their lives to make them honest and highly functioning people amid society with a moral compass.

Do not only believe in God but know that your walk with Him creates a personal relationship that no establishment and no individual should get in between.

From an early age, I witnessed the teachings of the Bible through my parents, specifically my mother, and all the benefits and trials that come with the territory. My siblings and I were taught how to pray and how to worship and love God with our entire beings.

In science we can do a brain MRI that can tell the difference between people who believe in God and people who claim atheism. The two scans have a stark difference. There is a void that can be seen in people who confess atheism. For people who believe in God, that void is not there; it's filled.

You can clearly see the difference with the emptiness being filled on the scientific level. There have been many things that I have seen my parents go without so that my siblings and I could have something. The fact that we are such well-rounded individuals is a testament to their faith. My mother, with the support of my father, opened up a school so that we could be exposed to the right crowd of people.

We had faith and also believed in God, which was a quality that was instilled in us, so that whatever our hands would touch would become prosperous and that whatever our minds believed, we could most definitely achieve it.

We owe all our success and our learning experiences to God our Father and to the vessels He has chosen to gift to us so that we might learn the truth and His power.

—Davielle Whymns

I have known Mrs. Darnell Whymns all my life. As her son, I have had the privilege to see her live from a true perspective that uniquely displays every detail of her character and growth fleshed out by the hand of God on her life. She has proven to be a remarkable woman, one not only of virtue but also of faith, true love, and patience. Her heart is seen by the many endeavors she has made to share throughout the years, such as leading youth groups, offering marriage counseling, serving as an educator, starting a faith-based education institution, and even taking a break from her personal pursuits to homeschool me, my siblings, and others for many years.

For more than twenty years, I have witnessed the consistency she has displayed through her entire life thus far. From her heart's passion, which lies in all forms of art, to her active lifestyle of faith, she has proven to be a resilient individual who has the ability not only to grow but also to influence others around her to grow positively toward Christ. This ability of hers to love others into becoming better individuals has forever changed my life. *Rough, reckless, arrogant,* and *harsh* are just a few mild words that describe who I was as a son, student, and person before I was gracefully counseled into being with Darnell's help. Through her character, example, and diligent counseling over many years, I not only have grown into an individual of integrity, strong morals, and faith but also have been an example to my peers and a person of kind heart.

There were many obstacles that I have been blessed to see and live through in the life of Ms. Darnell Whymns. Truly she is rightfully deserving of every merit. On countless occasions, the troubles of life—financial, physical, mental, emotional, and of course spiritual—contended with her faith, peace, and purpose. I have witnessed her overcome turmoil in all these areas for the sake of everyone but herself. I've seen her best poverty and despair when all her supporters in truth manifested to be nothing more than the very chains that tried to keep her from purpose. I have seen her overcome multiple sicknesses, traumatic life events, and even surgical procedures just so that she could live on to breathe life—spiritually, mentally, and emotionally—into others on her job, in her country, at home, and beyond. I am convinced that the great love, patience, and wisdom that has molded her through all her hardships in life will bless each reader, as the end result of all these has built her up to this point, which is perceived upon reading *Releasing the Overcomer's Anointing* and the many others to come. Amen.

—David Whymns Jr.

My mother. More like my inspiration, my life coach, my prayer interceder, and so forth. Not only because she gave birth to me and raised me to be the woman I am today, but also because while she was raising me, she showed me ways of how to live a godly, ladylike life. Whenever my sister and I sat down, our mother always taught us how to cross our legs at the ankle and sit up like the princesses we were meant to be. She influenced me to take these traits and many more with me on my journey abroad. But most of all she taught me how to fight the war in the spiritual realm. I remember when I was younger and she would sometimes disappear into her closet. A few minutes later I would hear shouting and praising. My mother influenced me to take up my Bible, go into my secret place, and show the enemy who is the boss—God. Her life has influenced not only her children but also all the people at her work and the school she ran. I'm sure all the kids who went to the school still remember my mother as the woman of prayer. When we prayed as a family and declared things in the spiritual realm, things would manifest in the natural. It was amazing. For example, when we had nothing to eat in our cupboards, my mother encouraged our family to open all the empty cupboards and start declaring miracles and blessings. Later that week, God came through and filled our cupboards with the groceries we needed.

—Danielle Whymns

REFERENCES

Deschene, Lori. "40 Ways to Let Go and Feel Less Pain." Tiny Buddha, 2021, http://tinybuddha.com/blog/40-ways-to-let-go-and-feel-less-pain/.

McLeod, S. A. "Information Processing." Simply Psychology, October 24, 2008, www.simplypsychology.org/information-processing.html.

Wikipedia, s.v. "Forgiveness." last modified 12 April 2021, at 00:06 (UTC) https://en.wikipedia.org/wiki/Forgiveness.

Printed in the United States
by Baker & Taylor Publisher Services